Praise for Boxtree's Motley Fool books:

The Motley Fool UK Investment Guide, amazon.co.uk's number one bestseller:

'(The book) is geared entirely to the UK market and it is difficult to see how anyone could fail to benefit.' *Mail on Sunday*

'…a thoroughly entertaining read… It shows the novice investor and the expert alike how to take full control of their investing future and how to have fun doing it.' *The Investor*

The Motley Fool UK Investment Workbook

'With its unique workbook format this is the most useful investment book of 1999.' *Mail on Sunday*

'Insightful, constructive and fun.' amazon.co.uk

The *Motley Fool UK* Web site is the winner of the 1999 *New Media Age* Award for Best Personal Finance Web site and the 1999 *Creative Freedom* Best Electronic Media Site

T0353420

The following Motley Fool books are also published by Boxtree:

The Motley Fool UK Investment Guide
The Motley Fool UK Investment Workbook
The Fool's Guide to Investment Clubs
How to Invest When You Don't Have Any Money: The Fool's Guide (available soon)

The Fool's Guide to Online Investing

Nigel Roberts with David Berger

B❋XTREE

First published 2000 by Boxtree

This edition published 2013 by Boxtree
an imprint of Pan Macmillan, a division of Macmillan Publishers Limited
Pan Macmillan, 20 New Wharf Road, London N1 9RR
Basingstoke and Oxford
Associated companies throughout the world
www.panmacmillan.com

ISBN 978 0 7522 6549 0

A CIP catalogue record for this book is available from
the British Library.

Designed and typeset by Anita Ruddell

Contents

Foreword

Nigel came on board as the third member of the Motley Fool UK, back in the hazy, early days of mass access to the Internet in Britain. Yes, we speak of an era as far back as early 1998!

Bruce Jackson and I had launched the Fool UK, an offshoot of its already famous older brother, the Motley Fool US, in late September 1997. It was an evening hobby for us after our day jobs were over, me as a doctor and Bruce as an accountant, and it wasn't long before we were badly in need of some help. We needed psychiatric help, of course, for having taken on such a mammoth task, but on a more practical level we also needed help on the site's message boards. Already at that early stage, too many messages were coming in for us to deal with them on our own and, besides, we didn't want to just deal with them ourselves. We hoped a community would develop which would be self-sustaining, in which everyone helped each other to learn about investing.

The growth of that community, we knew, was going to depend on some enthusiastic talents appearing on the message boards. These would be people who loved the concept, loved investing, spent far too much time at the Fool's site and who seemed to derive an unearthly joy in simply helping others out.

One day, we realized we'd been seeing a lot of a character called 'NGRoberts' posting on the boards. NGRoberts was enthusiastic, seemed to know a fair bit about investing and was stimulating a lot of discussion through his own postings. As time went on, he became one of the key figures in our developing community, so key in fact that we had to hire him. TMF Nigel, as he inevitably became, took on some of the writing commitment and also patrolled the message boards, nurturing discussion, helping newcomers and dealing with the occasional miscreant.

Two years on and now a Motley Fool veteran, you won't find anyone with a more detailed knowledge of online investing in the UK or a better understanding of what it all means to the individual investor. Nigel is the ideal person to write this book and I think you're going to enjoy it.

David Berger
Founding Fool
Motley Fool UK
London
December 1999

Introduction

Thinking about investing for your future? All too commonly, we feel ignorant and intimidated about investing, especially when it comes to dealing one on one with the professionals. Luckily for us, though, things have now changed. Completely.

Now, we can use the vast resources of all kinds which the Internet provides to decide exactly how we want to direct our financial futures. Eventually, when we're happy with our level of knowledge and understanding and have a clear idea of where we are aiming to go, the mechanics are as easy as Point, Click and Invest.

You'll often hear it said that the Internet offers everyone, investors especially, a mind-boggling amount of information. That's true. So much so, in fact, that it has now entirely levelled the playing field between private and professional investors. We hope *The Fool's Guide to Online Investing* will show you how to access that information and how you can take part in the amazing revolution that will change the way all of us secure our long-term futures. Information, though, is just one aspect of the breathtaking world which the Internet makes available to ordinary people. But, more compelling even than the volume of raw information at our fingertips, is the chance to organize that information in intelligent ways and the opportunity to learn the ins and outs of our subject to a depth we would never have believed possible.

And, here's the best bit: it's the *communication* possibilities the Internet places right in our laps which are the most breathtaking and which we suspect will fire you most of all when you come online.

Right here, right now, you have a global platform on which to express your thoughts. It's an awesome phenomenon. At its heart, the Internet is really a means of communicating, which allows both one-to-one contact (through e-mail) or one-to-many contact (through publishing something on a Web site) with almost equal ease. The publishing side of the Internet has some similarities to the traditional mass media, such as newspapers or television, but only some. The difference is that the Internet user – that's you – can as easily participate in creating the content as the professionals. Every week on our message boards at The Motley Fool UK we have thousands of messages from ordinary people who like to call themselves Fools, talking about all kinds of subjects. Each one of those people is publishing their thoughts in a world-wide medium and contributing to an endeavour at whose heart is an aspiration for self-improvement, a wish to escape from the pomposity we normally associate with money and, finally, a desire to smile once or twice along the way.

This two-way contact is tremendously energizing and gives instant feedback. In other words, if we publish something at our Web site and you don't agree with it, you can instantly e-mail us or post a message to that effect on one of our message boards, which will be available for the world to see. That also goes for you, of course, publishing your thoughts directly onto the message boards. It is an altogether unprecedented phenomenon.

Now, we did some thinking here at Fool HQ and it seems to us there are likely four types of people reading this:

1. Experienced investors who want to learn about the online world.
2. Experienced users of the online world who want to learn how best to use it for investing.
3. People who don't know anything about either subject, but are keen to learn.
4. Total klutzes who have no idea what we're talking about and were anyway looking for something on Szechuan cuisine. Here's how we think each of these groups should use this book:

1. All of Part 1 will be very relevant for you and help you get online. Hopefully, you'll find Part 2 illuminating. Parts 3 and 4 are an absolute must.

2. Do us a favour, will you? If you really know loads about this stuff, skip the bits of Part 1 which deal with the basics of getting online and the history of the Internet. It will just irritate you. Then you'll be in a bad frame of mind for the rest of the book, which would be a shame because the rest of it is relevant for you.

3. Unfortunately, you have to read everything. (And there'll be a test at the end with detention for those scoring less than 70 per cent.)

4. Tear up the book and use the pieces to light a fire under your wok.

One final thing: this book is not an exhaustive look at online investing. Rather, it's a 'fool's guide'. That means it represents the Fool's view, and much of it is obviously centred around the Fool's Web site. You won't find anything here on daytrading, options trading, warrants, futures, spread-betting or anything else which is more akin to gambling than investing. While the Internet has brought unprecedented opportunity into our homes, we firmly believe it hasn't changed the ground rules of common sense, and we aim to reflect that here. In other words, this is a book for long-term *investors*, not short-term *traders*.

Hopefully, you'll find this book packed full of useful information from the investing front line. If there's anything you feel should have been put in, but wasn't, or things which could have been improved upon, then e-mail us at **OnlineInvesting@fool.co.uk**. If we incorporate your suggestion into the next edition of this book, not only will we send you a free copy, but when you open it you'll find your name in flashing neon (or at least in the list of acknowledgements).

Chapter 1
Who are these Fools anyway?

'Invest me in my Motley – give me leave to speak my mind.'
William Shakespeare, *As You Like It*, Act 2, Scene 7.

The Motley Fool name harks back to the Fool of the Middle Ages, that character so beloved of Shakespeare, who was the only person who could tell the King the truth without getting his head chopped off. The Fool kept his head because he used humour to convey a sometimes unpalatable reality.

So what is the Foolish truth when it comes to finance?

Well, partly it's that the financial world preys on ignorance and fear. Throughout your life you'll have found financial professionals doing their best to sell you their own version of financial 'Wisdom', designed more often than not to benefit them rather than you. Meanwhile, personal finance and investing are not taught in any effective or consistent fashion in our schools. That means no one prepares you to manage your own finances, budget or stay out of debt. Even more importantly, no one introduces you to the wonders of compound growth and the importance of time, plenty of time, in investing. As a result of this lack of education most people grow up unaware of how to manage their money. They simply don't understand how to buy a house, buy a car, be responsible with their credit cards or invest in the stock market. None of these things should be a great mystery. In fact they are simple and mastering them leaves the individual in control and self-confident. However, without the proper education, they are intimidating, confusing and downright scary.

Because of this most people simply abdicate responsibility

for one of the most important aspects of their lives: their savings. Instead, they hand over their destiny to the people that Fools call the 'Wise'. They end up relying on an Independent Financial Adviser (IFA). There is a small minority (10-15 per cent) of IFAs who operate on a fee basis. However the vast majority of people who make their living in an office with 'IFA' nailed to the door are neither truly independent nor advisers. They are in fact salesmen for financial products on which they earn commission. While the name makes them sound like kindly people whose sole mission in life is to help maximize your savings, this isn't quite true. At least partly, their aim must be to maximize those commissions. That's natural because the commissions they receive from you are how they pay *their* mortgages. Unfortunately, it also presents them with a fatal temptation to sell investments which pay higher commissions. Fatal for you, that is.

Stockbrokers, banks and financial advisers often strive to present to you the image of their financial success, experience and utter respectability. At the same time, the reality of their actions in cynically selling their customers high-charging, under-performing investments is entirely at odds with this image. It is this anomalous behaviour which Fools know as conventional 'Wisdom'. The Wise have made enormous amounts of money from fools (note the small 'f') in the past, but times are different now and the peasants are revolting.

Most of us have been fools in the past. We have handed over a chunk of our financial future to people we trusted to give us advice. Many of us have bought endowment policies or invested in a unit trust (or other managed fund) which we were informed had 'returned above average of the funds in its sector'. We signed up and handed over our money. Only after the event did we discover that none of the funds in that sector had kept pace with the market index. Typically we discovered this at around the time when we realized that a slice of our savings was going to pay commissions to the purveyors of this poor advice. Oh, we were so foolish! When it comes to paying for education, somehow lessons in the importance of reading small print always seem to cost much more than other forms of learning.

Many of us at the Motley Fool have had these experiences. Indeed, these are the sort of things which made us want to be Fools in the first place – and the Internet is what made it possible. People often ask us exactly what Foolishness is all about and below are a number of principles which David Berger initially set out in the introduction to *The Motley Fool UK Investment Workbook*. They're not designed to be all-encompassing or exclusive, but simply to give a feel for the kinds of thing the Fool represents.

Enjoy Life

It is too short to get terribly serious about. It really is. So, while we love investing, that doesn't mean it has to be a dreadfully serious, worthy and – this was coming, you knew it was – *Wise* undertaking. Kick back, relax, have a laugh, be Foolish, for this is the Age of the Fool!

Part of enjoying life is being able to rest assured that you are providing adequately for your future. If, however, it becomes all-consuming, obsessive and to the detriment of other aspects of your life, then halt! You've got the balance wrong. Live well and enjoy life. If you have no room for a sense of ease, if your endeavours to grow your wealth have taken over everything – if you've missed the point of it all – then that's troubling and definitely not Foolish.

Nurture a Foolish Approach to Investing

You could call this a rational approach, but it wouldn't quite hit the spot. There's common sense and rationality in it, but also a slightly head on one side, contrary, skittish way of looking at things. As a Fool, you will also grow to be self-confident, comfortable in your own abilities and not cowed by the tactics of the financial services Mafia, aka 'The Wise'. Above all, our approach is long-term and aims to build wealth steadily and effectively over time. There are no get rich quick schemes to be found here. Begone hypesters and Johnny-come-latelys!

Sort Out Your Own Goals and Risk Tolerances

No one knows you like you do. Except your psychoanalyst. Your psychoanalyst, though, is unlikely to be involved in your investment decisions, so, until we can get our Foolish psychoanalytical service up and running, no one knows you like you do. That means that no financial adviser, no matter how 'independent' they may call themselves, can understand what your goals and ambitions and life philosophy are.

The Best Things in Life are Free

The velvet caress of a summer's evening. A joke shared with a stranger. Ideas and philosophy and the heady aroma of true liberation. *Der Fool! Der Fool ist* free! Or at least, pretty well free. You've paid for this book, possibly, but in some ways this is a 'value-added' service. The kernel of the Motley Fool's philosophy, a plethora of daily articles, a range of data services and the Motley Fool's thriving online community are available free to anyone with access to the Web. Crucially for us, that means we don't see ourselves as having a conflict of interest with the people who visit the site. We don't sell any financial services ourselves and currently have no plans to.

Get Out of Debt

Short-term, high interest rate debt in the form many of us carry it – on credit cards – is pernicious and nasty. It must be avoided at all costs.

The Power of Time and the Miracle of Compounding

One of the most popular chapters of *The Motley Fool UK Investment Guide* was entitled 'The Miracle of Compounding'. In it, we followed the fortunes of a variety of characters who saved different amounts over different periods of time. The conclusions are truly extraordinary and you'll find them summarized in Step Two of the Ten Steps at the Fool's Web site: **http://www.fool.co.uk**. If you really think you're not interested in this stuff at all, do yourself the favour of logging on and checking out Step Two first. Odds on, it'll make you reverse your decision.

The Power of the Stock Market
Over time, the stock market is the most reliable accumulator of long-term wealth available to us. There are many preconceptions and fallacies about it, but it is the place for Fools to grow their long-term money. No doubt at all.

The Power of the Individual
The average individual can indeed understand what investing is all about and can make investing decisions for themselves. Mostly, they do not need 'financial advice' and can learn to select their own investments with far less specialized knowledge than is generally believed. The mythology, fostered in large part by the financial services industry, that they *cannot* do so is a major contributor to the high level of ignorance and misconception about investing. This book and the Motley Fool aim to dispel this myth, enabling and enobling many ordinary people in the process.

The Power of Community
One of the major driving forces behind the success of the Motley Fool has been the community of people who use the site and post on its message boards. By their own contributions and the collective force that they represent, Fools using the site – that potentially means you – are as important in the day-to-day running of the Fool and shaping its future direction as are employed Fools. The Motley Fool only works because it touches people and helps them steer their lives for the better. That makes them want to give back to others and keeps the phenomenon surging forward.

Chapter 2

From Mr. Babbage to the Web: A Brief History of the Internet

Computers and the Internet are older than you think

Cyberspace, the World Wide Web, the Internet, online, are all words used to describe a new communications medium. Such new media do not come along very often, indeed the last big change was the mass adoption of the television. The online world is going to change all of our lives, but the revolution has only just begun.

The popular view is that the Internet is a new thing. Well, it is, isn't it? It's only in the last few years that the word 'Internet' has been tripping off everybody's tongue. In fact the very first message to be sent on the Internet passed from a computer in Los Angeles, to another in Stanford, California thirty years ago. The 30th anniversary of that first message occurred on 19 October 1999, while this book was in the final stages of editing. That message was to consist of three letters, 'L', 'O', 'G', spelling the first part of 'Login'. The system crashed, however, after only 'L' and 'O' had been transmitted, thus starting a tradition of computer crashes at the most irritating moment possible which has continued unbroken to the present day.

While the origins of the Internet go back thirty years, the exact origins of the computer are lost in the mists of time. Certainly, calculating machines of various sorts, with varying levels of automation, have been constructed down the ages and as with every other technological breakthrough, every nation claims that one of its own sons made the crucial leap. For the Scots it would be Napier, whose 'bones' were a precursor of the slide rule. For the French it would be Blaise Pascal for the seventeenth-century invention of a mechanical adding machine. In recognition of this, the programming language, Pascal, was named after him in the 1970s and was the introductory programming language for generations of professional programmers. For the Germans it would be Leibnitz, who produced a four-function calculator a few decades after Pascal. For the Irish it would be George Boole's work formalizing the laws of logic into what is still called 'Boolean Algebra' in his honour, laws which lie at the heart of the way all modern computers work.

The *real* inventor, however, was an Englishman called Charles Babbage. No, honestly! He is usually acknowledged as the first person to build a programmable calculating machine. That is, one which had a separate program of instructions which, once devised could be stored and carried out later. This is one of the defining characteristics of the modern computer. He designed his 'Difference Engine' in 1823 and his 'Analytical Engine' in 1834. Lady Ada Lovelace (daughter of Lord Byron, the poet) worked with Babbage and is usually acknowledged as the world's first computer programmer.

Unlike today's computers, Babbage's machines were built out of brass gears rather than silicon chips. The Difference Engine was put to work calculating mathematical tables. Babbage, who in his day job worked for the Royal Mint, went on to design the more general Analytical Engine, but sadly he never saw a complete Analytical Engine finished. There was not sufficient precision in the mechanical engineering of his day to machine the parts, but his great idea was sound. In the 1990s the Science Museum in London used Babbage's designs to build a complete Analytical Engine and, lo and behold, it worked!

Functioning mechanical calculating devices were, however, popular by the 1900s and punched cards and mechanical tabulating machines became increasingly common. It wasn't until the 1940s, though, that stored program electronic computers became a reality. Code-breaking during the Second World War provided the incentive for many of the breakthroughs. Everyone, surely, has now heard of the German Enigma machines and the code-breaking work at Bletchley Park that almost certainly knocked years off the war. This was the time when machines like ENIAC and Colossus earned their place in history.

In 1947 a team led by William Shockley at Bell Labs invented the transistor. This enabled the start of miniaturization and in recognition they were awarded the 1956 Nobel Prize for Physics. By the 1960s most major corporations had a 'Data Processing Department' staffed by digital high priests who tended their 'main-frame' computers in an air-conditioned inner sanctum far away from the owners of the data they were processing. They always showed these computer rooms in 1960s science fiction films like *The Andromeda Strain*. Remember? They looked like banks of fridge-freezers with flashing lights and huge whirring tape decks. Visitors would be invited to peer through the glass panel in the door, but never allowed to actually touch.

One of the exceptions to the general trend was the Ferranti Atlas computer developed in Manchester, as the 1950s turned into the 1960s. It had a 'timesharing operating system', which for the first time meant that users, many of them at once, could sit in front of keyboards to use the computer. They were allowed to use a terminal, made up of keyboard and screen, but not to actually touch the computer itself. If they wanted, say, a new reel of tape loaded, they would have to contact the high priests in the computer room. There was also a facility to send a message to the operators, or to other users, and before anyone had realized what was happening this most expensive of programmable calculating machines had become a communication device, a portent of things to come.

In the 1970s more and more of these terminals appeared

throughout the corporate and academic worlds. Of course no one had one at home. Meanwhile the trend for miniaturization continued. Gradually, the mainframes were replaced by 'mini computers'. Now, something the size of one fridge-freezer could do the work of what a few years earlier had seemingly required a whole shopful. The electronic development which made this possible was the Integrated Circuit (IC). These were little 'chips' of silicon with transistors etched upon their surface. In our modern chips-with-everything world they crop up everywhere from washing machines to mobile phones. The first ICs with a whole processor on a single chip appeared in the early 1970s. These 'microprocessors', as they were called, were what made the 'micro-computer' possible.

It was also the microprocessor which led to the first computer games appearing in the home. There was an 'electronic table tennis' machine released in 1972. I remember this distinctly because I had one for my eleventh birthday, and spent many, many hours hunched in front of the television knocking that little square back and forward with rectangular bats – dink, dink, dink-dink; dink, dink dink-dunk! No one else could use the television. It must have driven my parents mad!

Meanwhile, back in Bell Labs in 1972, two frustrated computer scientists, Thomson and Ritchie, felt that they were never given enough turns on the company's Big Computer. It was controlled by something called the 'Multics Operating System', one of those systems which allowed lots of people to share the same computer. In their frustration they locked themselves away and developed an operating system which would allow them to make use of a spare computer. As a joke they called their operating system 'Unix', as a pun on the name Multics and gave this operating system away to other researchers in labs and universities. In doing so, they created the first operating system which would function across computers made by lots of different manufacturers. They also created the 'open source' tradition where programmers place their programs in the public domain, requiring only that those who make improvements make them available through a central coordinator. Hence Unix became ubiquitous in computer science labs. It became not only the basis for the infrastructure of the Internet, but its development represented one of the first great collaborative efforts, efforts which are so typical of what occurs on the Internet to this day.

The actual invention of the Internet is credited to fear of mass destruction brought about by the cold war. A US think tank, aided by the RAND Corporation, posed the following question to itself: 'How could the US authorities successfully communicate after a nuclear war?' Post-nuclear America would need a command-and-control network, linked from city to city, state to state, base to base. But no matter how thoroughly that network was armoured or protected, its switches and wiring would always be vulnerable to the impact of atomic bombs. A nuclear attack would reduce any conceivable network to tatters. And how would the network itself be commanded and controlled? Any central authority would be an obvious and immediate target for an enemy missile, and the centre of the network would surely be the very first place to go. Well, the RAND thinkers thought about this in secret, as think tanks funded by the US military usually do, and arrived at a radical solution. They suggested that if the central authority was such an obvious target, why not have a network that would have no central authority? They suggested a network could be designed that would operate in a permanent state of anarchic self-regulation.

What IS the Internet?
The basic principles of the RAND idea were quite simple and represent a fundamental way of describing the Internet. The network would be presumed at every point to be unreliable. It would be made up of a series of interconnecting centres, or nodes, and each node in the network would be

ranked equal in status to all others. Each node would have its own authority to originate, pass and receive messages. The messages themselves would be divided into small portions, known as packets, with each packet addressed separately. Each packet would begin at some specified source node, end at some other specified destination node, and would make its own way through the network. The particular route that each packet took would be unimportant, and only the final reassembled message would count. Each packet would be handed on like the children's game of pass the parcel from one node to the next, in more or less the right direction, until it ended up at the correct destination. If parts of the network had been destroyed, that wouldn't matter; lost packets would be re-sent down a different route, passing from one node to the next surviving node until they reached their final destination. This overall system was known as packet switching.

Another way of looking at it, which emerged over the early years, was that the Internet could be regarded as being made up of layers. Three of the ones which are easiest to explain follow. The 'physical layer' was concerned with the actual cables connecting one point to the next, the 'circuit layer' with the entire route from the source computer to the destination computer and the 'application layer' had many different faces, each dealing with a particular aspect of the service.

This layered approach meant that new services could be added simply by defining the required protocol at the application layer. Baffled? Wait. Looking at the Internet like this puts in context much of the jargon users of the modern Internet hear bandied about:

The Post Office Protocol (POP) for obtaining e-mail.
The Simple Mail Transport Protocol (SMTP) for sending e-mail.
The File Transfer Protocol (FTP) for obtaining files from a remote computer.
The Hypertext Transport Protocol (HTTP) by which pages

21

of the World Wide Web are exchanged and viewed. That's why Web pages always start: http://. All these things are simply different protocols in the 'application layer'.

And now it's time for a bit more history. The National Physical Laboratory in Great Britain set up the first test network on these principles in 1968. This was followed soon after by a larger, more ambitious project in the USA, funded by the Pentagon. This became known as ARPANET, after its sponsor, the Pentagon's Advanced Research Projects Agency. This was the four-node network whose 30th anniversary we mentioned in the previous section.

ARPANET was eventually aimed primarily at helping to improve the use of scarce computing resources by enabling the sharing of computer power over the network. Remember, in the early 1970s, computers were expensive and rare. They therefore needed to be used to their full potential. By 1972 there were thirty-seven nodes, and the system had proved itself in its primary task of enabling the sharing of resources.

During the early years of ARPANET, something strange began to happen. The network users hardly bothered to use the power they had at their fingertips to share resources. Instead, they turned it into a glorified high-speed, and very expensive, electronic post office. The main use of ARPANET was no longer the long-distance computer sharing that it was originally designed for. No, the scientists were now using the system to collaborate on projects, to trade notes on work, and, most importantly of all, to gossip.

Each of the scientists had their own personal user account on the ARPANET computers, and their own personal address for electronic mail. In 1975, the idea of the mailing-list was invented, allowing an identical message to be sent automatically to large numbers of network users. Not surprisingly, perhaps, these scientists did not use this system to discuss mundane subjects and in fact the most popular of those early mailing lists was 'SF LOVERS', for science fiction fans. This was definitely not work-related and the bosses, as bosses have always done, tried to control it and stop it. Unfortunately for them, though, the very nature of the network made controlling it almost impossible.

Throughout the 1970s, ARPANET grew and its decentralized structure made expansion easy. As long as an individual machine observed the packet-switching protocol required to communicate, it could be situated anywhere in the world. ARPANET, being of military origin, was tightly controlled until 1983, when the military segment broke off and became MILNET. The software that controlled this new medium was now in the public domain and the growth therefore became uncontrolled, decentralized and anarchic. It was impossible to stop anyone anywhere in the world from linking up his or her computer to the network. The Internet was truly launched.

ARPANET as a body faded away in 1990, as other bodies took on the responsibility for administering the Internet.

What IS the World Wide Web?

In 1991, a new Internet-based service was developed at CERN (the European nuclear research centre). It used the idea of a 'hypertext' to make collaborative work easier within a group of researchers who were situated remotely from each other. The term hypertext referred to the fact that whenever one body of text mentioned another one, the reader was offered the opportunity to switch to reading the other one. Having read that they would then have the possibility of returning to the original. Hence, as you read one document you could pass from one to the next with ease and eventually find yourself working your way through the whole CERN library. In a way, their library had become one big interlinked document, or else a web of documents. Tim Berners-Lee, one of the engineers working on the project, coined the term 'World Wide Web' and the application layer through which most people now see the Internet came into being.

As with any other Internet service, the creation of the World Wide Web simply required the definition of a new protocol, in this case HTTP (the Hyper Text Transport Protocol). Once that was in place an HTTP server program could be written to manage the libraries of documents, and an HTTP 'browser' program could be created to give readers access to those documents. A person could then sit in front of a computer somewhere on the Internet, using the browser program to read documents from the library. The browser would send requests (in HTTP) to the server asking for such-and-such a document. The server would respond with 'here is document so-and-so' and 'this is what type of document it is', again all in HTTP. All of this sat as a new layer on top of the existing Internet services.

Berners-Lee and his colleagues developed the first server and browser programs, but within a year there were others. A browser called Mosaic, developed at the University of Illinois, soon established itself as the easiest to use. The Mosaic development team subsequently spun themselves off as one of the first high-profile Internet flotations on the stock market, known as the Netscape Corporation. Today, they are a part of the mighty AOL, one of the pioneers of mass Internet access through their America Online service.

Scale of the Internet

Currently, there are millions of nodes in the Internet, scattered over every country in the world, and the Internet represents freedom. There are no Internet police, there are no censors, no bosses. In principle, any node can speak to any other node, as long as it obeys the rules of the communications protocol.

In fact, thinking about the Internet communications protocols as the languages of the Internet is a good way to understand how it is uncontrolled and uncontrollable. Consider the English language. Nobody actually owns English. In fact, most people who speak English do not even live in England. Once you have learned to speak English you can make whatever use of it you wish. You can change it and create new words. English constantly evolves. A lot of people earn their living from using and exploiting English, but it is communally owned. Would English be improved if the 'The English Language' was owned only by the English who protected it and prevented it from evolving and changing? What if you had to pay a licence fee every time you used a word from an English dictionary, or had to obtain permission every time that you constructed a novel sentence using English™? It would be ludicrous. Like English, the Internet belongs to everyone and is controlled by no one.

There are now over 50 million host computers on the Internet and over 200 million users. In the UK there are well over 10 million users, representing over 20 per cent of the population. The number of WWW servers has grown from around 100 in its first year to over 7 million at the time of writing.

The number of users of the Internet is likely to reach over 300 million by the end of the year 2000, continuing the trend of doubling every year. But even then, that will still only account for about 5 per cent of the world's population. There's plenty of room for growth yet.

What Happens Next

'Convergence' has been a buzzword of researchers and technology watchers for the last decade. They are referring to telecommunications, computers and consumer electronics all coming together into information appliances. In the background is the talk of formats and protocols, licensing agreements and patent sharing. For the consumer we are already starting to glimpse the results in mobile phones from which we can read our e-mail, television set-top boxes on which we can buy things over the Internet and colleagues who insist on using their desktop computer as if it were a hi-fi. This convergence is making the Internet more attractive, more usable and more available, to the point where it will shortly be ubiquitous. In years to come the question 'Are you on the Internet at home?' will seem as incongruous as 'Have you got mains electricity?'.

Perhaps the most critical feature of the Internet is that it is a two-way medium, unlike previous mass media which allowed no real interaction. By allowing ordinary people to have their say it offers a global audience for voices that might otherwise never have been heard. It invites and facilitates multiple points of view and dialogue in ways impossible in the traditional, one-way media. For you personally, the Internet opens a world of unimaginable opportunity, not least when it comes to investing, so we'd better move on and see how to get you online.

Relevant Internet links:
Bletchley Park and the History of Computing – **http://www.cranfield.ac.uk/ccc/bpark/links.html#comphist**
The Charles Babbage Institute – **http://www.cbi.umn.edu/**
University of Manchester Celebrates Birth of the Modern Computer – **http://www.computer50.org/**
Understanding the past – **http://www.chaos.com/learn/History.html**
A Brief History of the Internet – **http://www.isoc.org/internet-history/brief.html**
Hobbes' Internet Timeline v4.2 – **http://info.isoc.org/guest/zakon/Internet/History/HIT.html**
The Roads and Crossroads of Internet History – **http://www.internetvalley.com/intval.html**
Internet Surveys – **http://www.nua.ie/surveys/index.cgi**

Chapter 3
Entering the Online World

Which Computer Do I Want?

In theory, we should be able to access the Internet from any old computer that has a modem (the device that hooks you up). In practice we are limited by the power of our system. If you have £1,000 to spare and were thinking of buying a computer, it is getting pretty hard these days to buy one that would *not* be Internet capable. Actually, it would be impossible.

So if you are going to buy a computer what are the bare necessities and what are the optional extras which you should consider? We will consider each of the following headings: memory, disk, monitor, modem and processor. In each case we will try to explain the basic idea, then give you some idea of the units in which they are measured and give you an idea of what you want to buy. Of course, people buy and use computers every day without understanding any of this stuff. If you're prepared to trust the spotty 12-year-old on the other side of the counter in your local computer shop to sell you the right thing, you don't need to read the rest of this section. If you want to have some idea of what he's talking about or might want to buy your computer directly by mail order, you do.

Predictably, the technology will probably have moved on for at least some of these factors by the time the book is published.

Memory – This is the computer's short-term memory, also known as RAM (Random Access Memory). Whatever is stored here is forgotten when you switch the computer off. It is measured in Megabytes (or MB). One of the letters on this page takes one byte to store. A Megabyte is a million bytes, so the whole of the text of this book probably takes up less than half a MB. However, the pictures take up more. (Remember they say that each one is worth a thousand words, and they ought to be because they cost more in disk space!) You should expect to be offered at least 32 MB or 64 MB these days. Any less is not a bargain, it's a problem.

Disk – This is the computer's long-term memory, generally referred to as its 'Hard Disk'. Things stored on disk stay around even if you shut the computer down and switch it off, and you save files to your hard disk and install programs on it. Typically, the disk will be about 100 times the capacity of the memory. This means they have to be measured in Gigabytes (GB), which are thousands of millions of bytes. You can expect to be offered between a 4 GB and a 10 GB hard disk. On a disk of that size you would have room to store hundreds of books like this one, including all the pictures. Any more is not a bargain, it's a white elephant.

Monitor – The monitor is the bit that looks like a television. However, because you are going to have this one right in front of your face, it ought to be better than a TV quality image. You want crisp, clear text and no flicker. Monitors are generally measured across the diagonal. Often you will be told that it is a '15-inch screen'. That means it has a 14-inch viewing area, as there is a dark unused margin around the outside. You want as much screen space as possible, but the big ones get expensive.

Modem – This is the device that allows your computer to be connected to the telephone system. It turns the digital signals used by your computer into sounds that can be transmitted over the phone line. Modems are measured in terms of the number of 'bits' which they can transmit in a second. Typical speeds are 28 thousand bits per seconds (known to the spotty youth as 'a 28K'), 33 thousand bits per seconds ('a 33K') or 56 thousand bits per second ('a 56K'). So what is this 'bit' thing? Well remember the bytes which we mentioned when talking about disk and memory? Each byte is made up of bits. It takes 10 bits to transmit a single byte or letter. You will rarely be offered less than a 56K modem these days and it may be referred to as a 'V90' because that is the name of the international standard for that speed of modem. The modem is potentially the bottleneck through which everything from the Internet must be squeezed, so the faster the better. Remember the rule of thumb about the text of this book? It is about half a million letters so when we have finished it will take around a minute and a half (500,000 x 10/56,000 = 90 seconds) to send the text over to the publishers, and as for the pictures, they could take another ten minutes!

Processor – This is the 'brain' of your computer. It is the part with which it does the sums and moves the data around. What matters for one of these is which 'processor architecture' it uses and how fast its clock ticks. At the time of writing the current technology for processors is the Pentium III for PCs and the G3 or G4 processor for the Apple Macintosh computers. About every year the chip makers launch a new processor architecture. They always say that this year's model represents the final revolutionary breakthrough. (Which will usually last all the way through until next year's.) All other things being equal (and remember we said that), the 'clock-speed' of the processor may be used to compare one with another between these breakthroughs.

Clock speed is measured in Megahertz (millions of ticks per second). A typical clock speed these days is around 300MHz. The spotty youth behind the counter will probably say things like:

'We've sold a few of those, but of course it's not as nippy as the 400 Meg, and it's only £50 more.'

or

'That's the same speed as the latest model from Dell and ours is only half the price!'

Here's a useful bit of verbal self-defence for just this sort of situation. Remember the 'all other things being equal' at the end of the last paragraph? Well tell him this: 'It is spurious to compare clock speed without regard to processor architecture. That's like you telling me that your lawnmower does more revs per minute than my BMW outside.' If nothing else he will be impressed by the notion that you have a Beemer in the car park.

Putting all the pieces together, unless you are going in for multimedia development and graphics (and you did say that this was your first computer, didn't you?), the standard hard disk is going to be easily big enough. So, on what, then, should you spend the extra money? First, a little extra memory. If you can get a bit more RAM fairly cheaply it is always worth upgrading. Really, though, 64 MB is plenty (or 128 MB if you really can't resist). If you are offered 64 MB of RAM as standard or you have more spare cash after upgrading, then think about screen space. The 17-inch monitors are coming closer to a consumer budget and you will probably appreciate more screen space before anything else.

Selecting your Internet Service Provider

Once you have your computer, the next thing to do is choose your Internet Service Provider (ISP). This is the company that acts as your gateway to the Internet via the telephone line. Until recently you would have expected to pay an hourly or monthly subscription for this service. Since the advent of Freeserve (the ISP launched by the electrical retailer, Dixons, in 1998), that is a thing of the past. There is no reason to pay for Internet access any more. Since Freeserve, a whole host of free ISPs have been launched, and it is now possible to get free Internet access from loads of companies, including Line-One, X-stream, and even Tesco.

You may find that when you take the computer out of the box it has been pre-configured to access some ISP with which the manufacturer has done a deal. If it's a free one that will probably do the job, but don't start keying in credit card numbers, just because there was an icon on the desk top. Alternatively, pick up one of the Internet magazines in the newsagents that will likely have a table comparing the major ISPs in the back. This will also have some blurb telling you what kinds of specific things to look for in your ISP.

How do free ISPs make their money? The way they mostly make money now is to split the price you pay for your local call with the telephone company concerned. In the future, some of them, Freeserve particularly, plan to boost their revenue by selling advertising on their site and selling products to you, the consumer, a practice known as e-commerce.

There are also some ISPs that are offering *entirely* free access via a freephone number. In this case, it is usually only at off-peak times, and there may be catches, such as one requiring you to switch your phone connection to their preferred supplier.

Most of these free ISP services are perfectly adequate, but beware that they do not provide free technical support over the telephone. This is another revenue stream for them, as for telephone help at a 'free' ISP you may have to pay a premium rate of 50p or £1 per minute. E-mail help and support is usually free.

Later, we will discuss the best way to set up your online identity, but for now it is not a bad idea to choose an ISP that allows you to have a number of different e-mail addresses. Most do.

Browsers, URLs, Hypertext, Links and Favourites
You will need to use a piece of software known as a browser. This is the program that understands and interprets the language of the Internet and shows it in the form of the attractively arranged words and pictures that you see on your computer screen. There are many different browsers out there, and some Internet buffs will tell you that their particular favourite browser is the best to use. If you have an old or what some may consider an underpowered computer, it may be worth considering one of the less well-known, but more lightweight browsers such as Opera or Lynx. In practice, most people will use one of the two most popular browsers, Internet Explorer from Microsoft or Navigator from Netscape (now owned by AOL). A browser can be a little

daunting to use at first, but once you understand the principles it becomes easier.

As with most things, the best way to learn is by doing, so get your computer set up, get online and play with your browser. But where do you start? Well as this is a Motley Fool book let's chance our arm and send you to the Motley Fool UK Web site. This is located (see below) at **http://www.fool.co.uk**, so how do you get there using your browser?

When you open up your browser, you may automatically be taken to what is known as your 'home page'. This is a page somewhere out on the Web. You can choose which page you want as your home page by altering the settings in your browser. How, though, do you specify precisely which page you want, as opposed to the other millions of pages on the Internet?

Let's pause for a quick fix of Internet jargon for a moment. You may hear the term 'URL' used by Internet geeks sometimes. This stands for 'Universal Resource Locator'. Clear, huh? Actually, this is just the correct technical term for 'address', the term most people use when referring to the location of a Web site. A Web site address or URL (the terms tend to be used interchangeably) looks like the Motley Fool address quoted above and usually starts with 'http' (for hyper text transport protocol – remember that in Chapter 2?). This is so common that if you leave it out the browser will put it in for you. (But if you are ever given a URL which starts 'ftp://' or 'https://' it is important that you include these.) Here are some examples:

http://www.yahoo.co.uk   A famous Internet 'portal' site.
http://www.bbc.co.uk   The BBC – a great site for
                               news.
**http://www.whyamIreadingabookonononlineinvestingamIs
omekindofsadandhopelessnerdorwhat.co.uk**

Back to home pages. Usually, your Internet Service

Provider, which often provides your browser, sets their own page as the default. For example, Freeserve likes you to see **http://www.freeserve.co.uk** as your first page every time you log onto the Internet and Microsoft's Microsoft Network (MSN) takes you to **http://www.msn.co.uk**. ISPs do this so that they can brainwash you with their content, flash ads at you and try to persuade you to buy various products which they, or their partners, happen to be flogging. That's OK, though. As we've seen, it's how they make money and provide you with a 'free' Internet connection. You don't have to take any notice if you don't want to.

Anyway, so there you are. You've launched your browser. It dials up and connects to the Internet. (Cue dial tone, lots of beeps and hisses and then silence as you are finally connected.) You're now taken to the browser's preset home page (see above). You're connected.

You're on the Internet!

Your hand shaking, lips a-tremble, heart beating in your breast, you spy a box near the top of the screen the cursor flickering gently in its left-hand corner. In Internet Explorer, this box is labelled 'Address' and in Netscape it is called 'Location'. You enter **www.fool.co.uk**, hit the return key, and then this happens:

Pretty, hey? We think so.

There are three sorts of things that you will find on a Web page:

1. Content – made up of text, pictures, animations, background sounds etc.;
2. Fields – where you may enter text;
3. Links (or 'click-ons') – including text (usually coloured and underlined to highlight it), pictures like the row of tabs at the top of the Fool page, or buttons. It's these which really make the Web a lot of fun.

Once the Motley Fool UK home page, as we fondly know it, has loaded, try moving the cursor around the page and you'll see that when it rests over some areas, it turns into a little hand with a pointing finger. That means the cursor is sitting over a 'link' (or a 'hyperlink') and if you click on it you will be transported to another part of the site. Try it and see. It's a lot of fun and makes navigation around the World Wide Web dead easy. You will also see text that is <u>underlined</u> here and there and this is usually another indication of a link that will take you somewhere else within the site, or somewhere else on the Internet.

Play around with your browser, see what it will do and get a feel for the basics. They're actually pretty self-explanatory and easy to use.

If you click on one of the hyperlinks on the Fool home page (or any other Web site) it will link straight to the next page. Sometimes this can be incredibly quick, and at other times it is infuriatingly slow. In reality, most linking on the Internet is quite fast, but as with a watched kettle, it can seem to take forever! But your browser gives you a wonderful tool which can be used with your mouse. If you are using Windows, you can 'right click' on the link, and you will be given the option to open the link in a new window (for Macintosh users, click-and-hold does the same thing.)

If you do this, the new page will open up in a separate window, and you can then click back to your original page and continue reading it while the new page is loading. This is a very powerful tool, and can be used extensively to speed up and improve your Web browsing. If you regularly visit a Web site that is very slow, you can open this one up straight away, and while it is loading up in the background, open up other pages that you might want. Then you can go back and read the first one at your leisure.

Once you have started to find your way around the Web, you will come across Web sites and pages that you want to go back and visit on a regular basis. These are your favourite sites, and you should add them to your favourites or bookmark list, depending on which variety of browser you're using. Once you have set this list up, you can access any of your favourite sites using the 'Favourites' menu of your browser in Internet Explorer, or 'Bookmarks' in Netscape Navigator, rather than having to type in the address manually every time.

It is well worth taking some time to organize your favourites or bookmarks into a rational order. It can be very tempting to simply keep adding more and more sites, but it can be difficult to remember what was what. You can set up new folders in your favourites list, into which you put individual favourites, according to how you want them classified. This lets you keep better control of what is, after all, your personal A to Z of the Web. A list of such folders might look something like this:

Investing Information sites
News sites
Share prices
Banking
Company Web sites
Brokers
Weird and Wonderful
Search Engines
Etc.

Security

There are two types of security risk when using the Internet. The first is that someone might intercept your information in transit, the second is that someone might impersonate you in order to access some private information or carry out a transaction in your name. Rest assured, neither happens very often. The use of passwords protects against impersonation. The use of encryption systems protects against information being intercepted in transit.

Choosing Passwords

The aim in choosing a password is that it should be easy for you to remember but difficult for someone else to guess. So don't use things which have an obvious association with you. Your first name as your username and your surname as your password is an outstandingly bad idea, but there are many other ways to get this wrong.

Really Bad Choices for Passwords

Remember that hackers – people who try and break into secure areas on the Internet – have computers too, so you should avoid things which are easy for a computer to guess. Nothing which occurs on a list is a good password, so a proper name is a bad choice, and any word which might be in a dictionary is a bad choice. Things which are easily generated are a bad idea, so a date is out. For example, if you choose your password from any six characters then there are a lot of choices (256^6 = about three hundred, million, million). However, choose a word from an average dictionary and there are only 60,000 of them, making the hacker's job so much easier. If you were to use a date in the last 50 years as your password you are reducing the options to around 18,000 (365 days x 50 years = 18,250). When we come down to your mother's first name – unless she's from Finland or Mongolia – then it is one of the 3,000 in the *Book of Girls' Names*. Be canny!

Good Practice for Passwords

Here are some suggestions that may help you generate a better password:

– Include numbers and non-alphabetic characters, like $,£, %, ! and &.

– Make it as long as is practicable.

– If you have to use a word or name then deliberately misspell it, or include special characters in the m!ddle.

– Don't write down your password but perhaps write yourself a crossword clue with the password as the answer.

– In order to cope with multiple, changing passwords, think up a systematic way for creating them. We won't give a complete example here, because people might copy it and that would be a hacker's dream, but we can outline an idea used by a certain nameless colleague of ours at the Fool. He uses a combination of numbers and words based on the titles and positions of books on the bookshelf next to his desk. (We've told him his cleaning lady will come in one day and rearrange them, but he won't listen.)

– Change your password regularly.

Sense of Proportion

All sorts of services on the Web will give you a username and password. For many of these you have very little to lose if someone else were to impersonate you. Thus, it doesn't much matter if someone reads your favourite free newspaper on the Web using your username and password. What this means is that you don't have to worry about creating hard to crack passwords for low security activities. Save your ingenuity for activities which really matter, like your brokerage account or bank account.

If you have any information which is very important and very private then copy it to a removable medium (a Zip or floppy disk) and lock it away. There are few computer security systems which will be more reliable.

Security and your Online Broker

We talk about brokers later, but your online broker will generally demand offline identification in order to open your account. In other words, they won't open an account without sending something by post (we Internet jocks call that 'snail mail') to your home address to check you really are who you say you are. They will normally only allow cash to be withdrawn from your account by posting a cheque to your home address. It is important that you keep this up to date, and it would give you peace of mind if they only allowed changes to this address after some conventional form of paper confirmation, such as a utility bill, had been produced. This would mean that even if someone was to break into your online brokerage account and see your portfolio, it might be embarrassing for you to know that they had seen what terrible shares you have selected, but it wouldn't endanger your money.

Encryption and Transactions

Encryption can be used both for transactions and for e-mail. When you are carrying out an important transaction on the Web you could check that the URL starts 'https' (rather than the usual 'http'). If it does then this indicates that the transaction is being handled by a 'secure server' which is using encryption. This extra security slows things down, so usually it is only applied to the page on which you give or receive private information. For example on the shop at the US Fool site (known as Foolmart), it is only the checkout page **(https://www.foolmart.com/market/shipping.asp)**, where the customer gives a credit card number, which is handled by a secure server.

Encryption and E-mail

Most people ignore the fact that their phone conversations may be overheard by any number of telephone engineers. Similarly your e-mail may be read by all manner of system administrators and engineers. In general it is good practice not to send anything by e-mail unless you would be happy to have it printed out and pinned to a public notice board. In fact, next time you are tempted to send a torrent of vitriol via e-mail (not that you do such things), consider that most e-mail can be read by a skilled hacker if they are determined enough. On the flip side, though, there's an awful lot of e-mail flying around the world and why are they interested in yours?

If you do need your messages to be absolutely secure, you could consider using PGP (Pretty Good Privacy). This is a free encryption system and the international version is available from here: **http://www.pgpi.org/**

Only very few people need this level of security, though, and you would need to check whether your correspondents are prepared to accept a message in such a format. The usual procedure is that they send you their encryption key and you send them yours and then all future messages are encrypted using the respective keys. The reason why such systems work is that you each keep secret the decryption key which you use to unpack the encrypted messages when they arrive.

A Note of Reassurance

You should not let these words about security put you off. The Internet is a very secure medium if you just take a few precautions, which is all this section is about. The actual likelihood of anyone gaining access to any of your private information is very small indeed.

Spam, Spam, Spam, Eggs and Spam

The reason some Web sites exist is to simply collect a list of e-mail addresses that they can then sell on to others to use in their marketing promotions. You want to avoid these sites and it's actually not that difficult to recognize them with a bit of practice. You will find, though, that once you do start to give out your e-mail address to various sites, many offering useful services which you do value, you will be bombarded with useless messages offering get rich quick opportunities and sex, sometimes both together. Also, if your e-mail address is published out on the Web, say on your Web site, you will find yourself getting a lot of this stuff, which is known as 'spam' in Internet jargon. The name comes from the Monty Python sketch where the choice was loads of spam with everything or... loads of spam with everything. Spam is an inevitable part of Internet life, in the same way as junk mail through your letterbox is an inevitable part of modern life. Neither of these things will hurt you, but they are annoying. There are a number of ways to minimize spam. These include not publishing your e-mail address on your personal Web site and giving out your e-mail address only sparingly on the Web. In practice, you will always receive spam and probably the best way around it is to filter it out by using a number of different e-mail addresses, as we look at in the next section.

How Many E-mail Addresses Do I Need?

If you want a very simple life, you can make do with one. However, if you have a work-related e-mail address, you might want to consider also getting another one for your personal use. This is so that you don't have to give all your friends a new e-mail address when you change jobs. It also means there is no chance of your boss seeing the e-mails you've been exchanging twenty times a day with a recruitment agency in your quest for a better job than the crummy one you have now. ('Thinking of leaving are we, Jenkins?' Ouch!)

Let's talk spam again. If it bothers you and you want to avoid it, having a third, low security, 'couldn't really care less' e-mail address can make a lot of sense. This is the e-mail address which you give out to all those Web sites which ask you to sign up to receive e-mail updates or to view particular content. You won't have to check it very often. Don't use this one for other functions like accessing your bank account or communicating with your friends. You'll find that this third e-mail address does absorb a lot of the spam, although you will find some will filter through to all your e-mail addresses eventually.

Here's how the e-mail addresses are shaping up then:

1. Work e-mail address: **fiona@deadendjob.co.uk**. Use this one for your job. Don't use it for private e-mails which you wouldn't want your boss to see.

2. High security personal e-mail address: **fiona@fionasisp.co.uk**. Use this for your bank account, any credit card transactions on the Internet and communicating with your close friends. Choose a savvy password and change it regularly.

3. Low security personal e-mail address: **fionababy@fiona-sisp.co.uk**. Use this for all those places on the Internet where they ask you to give out your e-mail address and although you quite want what they're offering, you say to yourself: 'Oh yes! What are they going to do with this e-mail address, I wonder?!' This address will get spammed. Since you don't check it very often, you don't really care.

One final note on e-mail addresses. At the Fool we do not make our mailing list available to anyone else. That means Fool users don't get spammed because of the Fool.

Searching the Web

The network is now huge, and there is so much information out there it can be very difficult to find exactly what you are looking for. This is where search engines come in handy. Search engines bring order to the Internet and it is worth taking some time to learn how to use them properly. In the appendix of this book we list many of the well-known search engines. Your use of the various search tools on the Web will be enhanced by knowing how they were actually designed, and especially by knowing the specific rules they use. These can be very different. If you access one of the search engines there will be an explanation of how it works somewhere on the site and it really is worth reading this.

Yahoo! is often said to be the best known of the search engines, but in some ways it isn't really a search engine at all. It uses human-sorted search categories (yes, real people do the categorizing), which is a unique offering in the Internet cataloguing world. It acts as a sort of Internet librarian which reads Web pages and can point you to a few which may be what you're looking for. A dozen other companies, including Lycos, Excite, Infoseek, and AltaVista, have all been trying hard to develop cheaper, faster, fully-automated Internet searching techniques that can match human judgement. They're getting better and better at it too.

Everyone has their own favourite search engine and I'm going to let you into the secret of my current one: Google. You'll find this at **http://www.google.com**. It prioritizes search results according to how many other pages it has found that link to the page in question, and thus can roughly judge how important or authoritative the rest of the people using the Internet consider that page to be. The results I get are so good that I hardly ever use another search engine now.

Another interesting search site is **http://www.askjeeves. com**, which allows you to enter natural language questions such as 'where can I find great information about UK shares?'.

Try a few different search engines for yourself. You will soon find which ones suit you and develop a list of your own favourites. You will then be in a position to enthral your friends with the differences and advantages of the one over the other. They will appreciate your sharing of this hard-won wisdom and love you all the more for it.

Newsgroups

Newsgroups operate a little bit like an open meeting place where conversations take place. There are literally thousands upon thousands of newsgroups, covering every subject you can possibly imagine. They are mostly unregulated, but that doesn't mean they are necessarily a free-for-all. The communities which spring up via newsgroups usually do a pretty good job of keeping them running smoothly.

News is another service with its own protocol (remember those protocols in Chapter 2?). The news messages are passed around the Internet using this protocol. Copies are kept by each server along the way. Your ISP will provide a separate server for news, where the originals of your messages and those of your fellow customers are kept. Copies of messages from readers of every other news server will be sent there also. In comparison to the bespoke message boards at the Motley Fool, newsgroups have less of a 'sense of place'. Perhaps more noticeably they don't have a resident group of Fools patrolling them to look out for the interests of the new people. It can seem a bit like the Wild West. However, there are a lot of people out there who use and love them.

The world of newsgroups is a complicated one, and well beyond the scope of this book. But if you call up the trusty Google, or any other search engine, and enter the words 'UK newsgroups' you will find links to many, many sites that can give a much better explanation of their use than we can here.

DejaNews which has recently changed its name to Deja.com (**http://www.deja.com**), is a site that specializes in cataloguing and searching through newsgroups and may be worth a visit if this interests you.

Viruses

Many viruses, which are simply computer programs passed from one machine to another, hidden inside other programs or documents, are harmless. A few, however, can have devastating effects, even destroying all the data on your hard disk. Certainly, reading a plain text e-mail message cannot transmit a virus to your computer.

There is another sort of virus where the message itself is the virus, although it is not harmful in any way. These e-mail messages always have a certain style and generally invoke authority: for example, 'We have heard today from

43

Compaq'. They warn of dire consequences if you open an e-mail with a certain title, and they insist that you tell as many people as possible. These are almost always hoaxes and passing them on simply makes you look silly to the more experienced Internet users.

If you download a program or file from the Internet, you should be wary about opening it, even if it comes from a source that you trust. The same applies if you receive a document attached to an e-mail message. People often pass on viruses without knowing that they are doing so. If you receive a file, such as a word processor document, which unexpectedly asks if you would like to run a macro (a small program embedded within the document itself) as you open, beware! Hit the 'NO' button (in fact, it might be the 'Disable Macros' button), delete the file and warn the person who sent you the document that you think they might have a virus.

It is well worth investing in a virus checker, and there are many out there. To learn more about viruses have a look, at **http://kumite.com/myths/** and **http://www.drsolomon. com/home/home.cfm**.

It is rare for your computer to be infected by a virus, but it is sensible to take precautions and always be wary of accepting unsolicited downloads from the Internet.

Relevant Internet Links
Google – **http://google.com/**
Ask Jeeves – **http://www.askjeeves.com/**
Yahoo! – **http://www.yahoo.co.uk**
Lycos – **http://www.lycos.co.uk**
Excite – **http://www.excite.co.uk**
Infoseek – **http://www.infoseek.com**
Newsgroup Search – Deja.com - **http://www.deja.com/**
Virus News – **http://kumite.com/myths/**
Norton Anti-virus – **http://www.drsolomon.com/**
Guard Dog – **http://www.cybermedia.com/products/ guarddog/gdhome.html**

Chapter 4
Foolish Basics I: The Real Basics

Investing online involves the same general principles as investing offline. There is no doubt that the online variety has many advantages over the offline, but the core principles remain the same. It's no good adopting a different investment style, or throwing sensible principles to the wind, simply because you're investing online. That's not where the magic of online investing lies. For that reason, in this chapter and the next, I am going to take a look at some Foolish basics. I'm not going to go into a huge amount of detail, just set the scene for where and why we should be investing. For a more in-depth look at Foolish investing than you'll find here, which just gives a very quick overview, take a gander at **www.fool.co.uk**, or even (sharp intake of breath!) stump up a few more quid for *The Motley Fool UK Investment Guide*, also published by Boxtree. The *Investment Guide* also deals in some detail with pensions, endowments, PEPs, ISAs and the like, which we don't deal with here. People who want a very practical approach, with a fair amount of depth in interpreting company accounts, on the other hand, may be more interested in *The Motley Fool UK Investment Workbook*, again published by Boxtree. What you'll find here is just a taster.

Are you sitting comfortably? Then we'll begin…

We've all seen it happen many times. There's a bit of turbulence in the stock market, it becomes quite volatile (the value of shares moves around a great deal in a short time) and maybe shares fall consistently for three days, a week, two weeks. At the first sniff of uncertainty the conventional media piles in with headlines like these:

40 Billion Pounds wiped off the Footsie!
Investors Scramble to Sell!
The Crash of 19?? (insert the year of your choice here)
Shares Carnage!
SELL!!

This kind of alarmist trash sells newspapers and attracts viewers. We're not knocking the conventional media [*Editor's note: Yes we are*.]. They have to make a living, after all. But this information does not represent the true facts of stock market investing as they have been played out over the years of this century.

Fool aficionados will have heard us refer many times before to the Barclays Capital Gilt Equity Studies. Rest assured, these research analyses are not required reading for aspiring Fools. Knowing some of the breathtaking information in them is, however, and we never lose a chance to bang on about it. Each year, Barclays Capital, a merchant bank, looks at the performance of equities (that means shares), as compared to cash in a deposit account and gilts (UK government bonds, which are the nearest to 'risk-free' investments there are). Reading and digesting the next few paragraphs, which contain some of the key points of the 1998 and 1999 studies, may change your view of investing entirely. If you were convinced that the stock market was the place to invest for the long-term anyway, these numbers may well reinforce that belief to the point of zealotry. You will become a bore to your long-suffering friends and relatives.

Was that enough of a build-up? You ready for this? You ready for what comes next? Sure? OK…

£100 invested into the stock market in 1918, according to the 1999 Barclays Capital Equity Gilt Study, would have been worth £1,000,351 today[1]. That works out at an average annual return of 12.2 per cent. Meanwhile, playing it 'safe' and putting your money into gilts would have transformed your £100 into a

---

[1] Disregarding the effect of inflation or taxes and with all income from dividends reinvested.

mere £13,315 over those eighty-one years. Putting it into a cash deposit account would have netted you just £7,038.

Savour those numbers for a while. The difference between them is extraordinary.

Still, the stock market is riskier, isn't it? You're more likely to lose money in the stock market than in gilts or cash, aren't you?

That is undeniably true, but there are two things to consider. Firstly, the stock market returns are not just a bit more than gilts or cash, they are phantasmagorically more, mega-more, mammothly more, really a lot, lot more. In other words, you are getting paid very handsomely to take risk. Secondly, there's risk and risk. Let's try and look at just how much risk you're taking by investing in the stock market.

In the 1998 study, Barclays Capital looked at all the rolling five-year periods since 1918 (1918-1923, 1919-1924, 1920-1925, you get the picture). During that time, they found equities had outperformed cash in 83 per cent of them. For gilts, it was 81 per cent. For consecutive ten-year periods, the numbers rose to 97 per cent and 96 per cent respectively. In other words, since 1918, money in equities has stood a greater than 80 per cent chance of outperforming cash and gilts over any five-year period and a better than 95 per cent chance of outperforming them over any ten-year period.

In other words, the stock market itself may be risky in the short term, but not in the long term. That doesn't mean, of course, you can't lose money by making poor investments, but it does mean the stock market is the best place to grow your long-term wealth. How to make good investments is one of the things we spend a lot of time looking into at the Motley Fool.

It's easy to get sucked into worries about when to buy and when to sell, and many investors try to time the market, attempting to buy whenever things are down and sell when they are up again. But trying to time the stock market is very hard indeed. A couple of chapters down in the Foolish Investing Guidelines, there's an example of just how hard it is.

So we need the ability to switch off from the day-to-day movements of share prices and not worry too much about them or the stock market as a whole. That doesn't mean we mustn't keep an eye on what is happening to our investments, or resolutely ignore all market news, just that we shouldn't get either too elated at short-term rises or distraught at short-term falls. One potential pitfall of online investing is that the availability of near instantaneous information can feed an unhealthy obsession with the unpredictable and meaningless short-term.

Yes, we speak of none other than the Daytrading **BOGEY-MAN**! This humanoid individual is unable to switch the market off. In his most extreme form, *Daytradimus*[2], to give him his scientific name, will trade the same shares many times a day, aiming for a quick profit each time and will hold only cash overnight.

It is impossible to predict with any degree of consistency what the market will do over a period of months, let alone minutes, making this practice little more than gambling. He, of course, pays a commission each time he buys a share and each time he sells one and is further hit by the difference in pricing between the buy and sell prices, known as the bid-offer spread. In addition, in the UK he has to pay 0.5 per cent of the purchase cost each time in stamp duty.

The Daytrading Bogeyman is currently under study by Professor Erhard von Kartoffelkopf of the Motley Fool Institute for Investment Anthropology. He wonders if the Bogeyman is actually a variant of the Himalayan Yeti or North American Sasquatch. Interesting theory. We'll let you know the outcome.

In the meantime, don't let the Bogeyman get you! Instead, think long term. Think of the way in which just £100 was turned into a million pounds through the work of Old Father Time and the stock market. Think of how badly you will hurt your returns by trading and trading and trading and how unlikely you are to be able to time the market with any degree of accuracy. It really doesn't pay.

---

[2] His full scientific name is *Daytradimus unhygenus*. Why so unflattering? Because he doesn't dare log off for anything at all. Approach wearing a Nuclear-Biological-Chemical Warfare suit.

Chapter 5
Foolish Basics II: The Index Tracker

In this chapter, we'll go through some more of the basics of Foolish investing. It's quite possible that many people will not need to go into much more depth than this and may not even want to look into investing in individual companies at all. That's OK. You haven't wasted your £5.99. You will have gained a clear focus of where you need to direct your energies and have a fair idea of how you want to go about doing that.

Before we get on to more general things, though, this is my book and so you're going to have to suffer my own foolish story.

Nigel's Own Foolish Story
At this point I have to confess I have not always been Foolish. Far from it. For many years I was quite happy to hand my own money over to 'the experts' to manage. After all, I did not have the time or the inclination or the ability (or so I thought) to manage it myself. How could I, some chap working away by himself, ever be able to understand the complexity of the financial world? Surely these experts could do a much better job at looking after my money than I would ever be able to do?

In 1987 I left the safety of my full-time senior manage-ment job to start my own business. I did not really have the time to think about my own investments so I contacted a Financial Adviser (who had been highly recommended by my accountant) to ask his advice about what I should do with my company pension. It took my 'oh, so nice' Financial Adviser no time at all to tell me that I should immediately transfer this to a personal pension. He produced lots of won-derful projected figures and graphs, which showed how my pension would grow and grow, and how I could easily be able to afford to retire by the time I was fifty.

I wanted to know the best place for me to transfer the pension to, and, without hesitation, he told me that his firm was 'very bullish on Japan'. When I said that I had read somewhere that the Japanese stock market was heading for a fall, he said, yes, he had read that too – but if this did happen it would create an incredible buying opportunity.

My 'oh so nice' Financial Adviser tried to persuade me to put 100 per cent of my transferred pension into Japan. But I resisted. 'OK, let's compromise,' he said. 'How about putting 50 per cent of the funds into Japan,' his firm were very bullish on Japan, you see 'and the balance into UK equities?' 'OK,' I said, 'that is a good idea. But which UK equities?' He said that after Japan, his firm were very bullish on smaller companies, and recommended that I put the balance of the funds into a UK smaller companies growth fund. Yes, a growth fund – that did sound good. I wanted my funds to grow, you see.

For the first three or four years, when I used to get my statements from the pensions company I would phone up my 'oh so nice' Financial Adviser. I would say that I was very disappointed with the performance of the funds. The UK smaller companies fund had grown a little, but the Japanese fund had fallen. 'Don't worry,' he used to say. 'You see my firm is very hot now on Japan. Think of the buying opportunity...'

It is now over eleven years later. I do still have that pension fund that was invested fifty-fifty in Japan and in UK smaller companies, only now the split of the fund is only 28 per cent Japan and 72 per cent UK smaller companies. You see, the Japanese fund is worth almost exactly what it was all those years ago, and the UK smaller companies growth fund is worth just over double.

The total pension fund is now worth 50 per cent more than it was eleven years ago. That has given me a staggeringly poor 4.5 per cent annualized growth for my fund each year, an amount which has hardly even kept up with inflation. Based on this it will be a long, long time before I can retire.

Luckily I had some Foolish tendencies long before I realized what a Fool was and I began to make separate provision for my retirement based on my own judgements. Nevertheless, I have kept these funds running to remind me what a desperate fool I once seemed to be.

Once I had realized that by devoting just a little bit of my own time and money I could look after my own finances quite successfully, I can safely say I had become a Fool. I was no longer compelled to line the pockets of those 'oh so nice' Independent Financial Advisers.

I soon learnt that the biggest problem I had in managing my own finances was that I lacked information. I spent years trying to gather enough information to enable me to make informed decisions, but as an enthusiastic amateur, I always found it difficult to keep up to date. Then about five years ago I discovered the Internet, and found out that there was information available out there, if only I knew how to find it. Then, two years ago, the Fool came into my life – what a revelation that was – here was a community of amateur investors, just like me.

The availability of investment information on the Internet grows daily. You can now access share prices and breaking news, and the amount of, and quality of, information available will continue to increase in the days and months ahead.

But being online is not just about information. As we've seen, it's about communication.

We are now rapidly moving into the communication age. Using our computers, we can communicate with hundreds of other people. We can ask questions, we can discuss ideas, we can share information. For now, though, let's take a look at some more of the really basic stuff, stuff you don't even have to have a computer to figure out.

Boring Stuff We All Need to Know

Investing in the stock market can be fulfilling and fascinating. Fools and would-be Fools reading this are probably itching to get on to the juicy parts of this book, the bits that deal with actual investing. In fact, the real hotheads have probably skipped most of the boring stuff already, opened an online brokerage account and been in and out of Freeserve eight times already today.

That's hopefully a bit of an exaggeration, but at this point we do need to shout 'HANG ON A SECOND! There something important to say.' Did that catch people's attention? Mmm, perhaps not, lets try that a bit louder:

'HANG ON A SECOND!'

Right, that's better!

You have put away a few pounds into a savings account (making sure that you are getting the highest rate of interest, of course) and you're thinking of starting to get maybe just a little bit more Foolish. You have already surfed around the Motley Fool Web site, and you have been posting messages on the Ask a Foolish Question message board. You want to be a Fool and you just can't wait to get on with it. Well, take a deep breath and slow down a bit. The biggest mistake that most new investors make is that they rush in and buy shares too quickly.

To be a true blue Foolish investor means you FIRST need to ensure that your personal finances are in good working order before you even consider buying any shares. As you'll find the Fool imploring again and again, do NOT rush; sort out your personal finances first. You know what's coming next, don't you? If we're bandying about phrases like 'sort out your personal finances', that can mean one thing and one thing only: get rid of your debt, young (old) Fool.

Credit Card Debt: It's a Killer

First of all, are you *routinely* setting aside an adequate percentage of your wages to put into your savings every payday?

Or do you only set aside money when there is something left over? Or worse, are you finding there is nothing left over at the end of every month? Maybe you're even going into the red, or perhaps it's got so bad that you've been relying on your flexible friend and not paying off the balance each month?

If you answered yes to any of the last three questions, you're simply not ready to start on this investing lark just yet. It's time to examine why you aren't saving money each month. A Fool does not go investing with their housekeeping money, or next month's mortgage, or with money that should go toward paying off a credit card. We invest money that we have worked for (or even with money we have not worked for – we're never too proud to accept gifts) and have Foolishly saved. We only invest money that is *free of any other obligation.*

In general, we suggest a good thing to aim for is to save around 10 per cent of your annual income. Some might manage only 5 per cent. Others might put away 20 per cent. It does not really matter how much, and the last thing we'd suggest is saving so much there is no joy left in your life, but the important thing is to establish a regular habit of saving and stick to it.

Next stop – have a look at your wallet or purse. How many credit cards do you have? Do you use one until you reach your limit, then swap to another? One of the most important principles of Foolish investing is to use only money that is free from any other obligation. This means that if you are carrying a balance over on your credit card every month then any money you have sitting in a bank or building society, which you may have saved to start investing, isn't free of obligation. And neither are you!

Here's why: many credit cards have an annual interest rate of over 20 per cent. I have just checked the rate of interest that I pay on my credit card balance (or would do, if I didn't pay it off every month) and it is currently 1.527 per cent per month. Now 1.527 per cent a month doesn't sound like a lot, does it? Well, imagine if every month you carry over £1,000 on your balance, that means that you pay interest of £15.27. Most cards require a minimum monthly payment of 5 per cent, so let's assume that you pay off enough each month to make at least the minimum payment and maintain the balance at £1,000. In a year you would pay interest on that £1,000 of £183.24 – or 18.3 per cent.

Meanwhile, if you had £1,000 invested in the stock market, it is obvious that you would have to achieve a return of 18.3 per cent *just to break even* on that £1,000. The average return on money invested in the stock market over the last eighty years is a little over 12 per cent per annum, so what chance do you have of actually achieving over 18 per cent on a regular basis? Using credit cards as a way of borrowing money is easy, too easy, and carrying credit card debt from one month to the next is simply foolish.

Credit card debt is a huge and largely hidden problem. It has been estimated that in the UK there are about 37 million credit cards[3]. About £20 billion of credit card debt is carried over each month and with 20 million households in Britain, that gives an average of £1,000 per household. With each of those households paying about 20 per cent per annum in interest on that debt, we're all in the wrong business...

Credit card debt is probably the major single reason why people struggle to manage their finances. If you can't manage to pay off your credit card balance each and every month then get out a pair of scissors, sit down at the kitchen table and get cutting. Then concentrate on ways of paying that debt and/or refinancing it at a lower rate, such as through a personal loan from your bank.

If you are able to manage your credit card so that you pay it off each month it can be a good way of spreading your expenses. You might even get a few perks such as bonus points or air miles. That's all fine. We all like the odd little freebie, but don't let your card take over your life, which it will if you don't keep it paid off.

---

[3] This data comes from **http://www.ccrg.org.uk/facts.html**

So, always pay off your credit card debts (and pretty much all other debts except your mortgage, which represents the lowest interest rate debt available) BEFORE you contemplate investing in the stock market.

A Good First Step: Index Trackers

If you're in the happy position of having your finances in order, having paid off all your debts and having enough saved-up money to fill an emergency fund of cash, should you need it, what should you do with the excess?

Many new investors will not immediately feel confident enough to go out and buy their own shares directly, so what should they do?

Many people in this situation choose to invest in a type of collective investment known as a unit trust. These are pooled investments in shares in which a fund manager generally tries to pick and choose which shares to buy in an attempt to provide the maximum investment returns. That sounds pretty reasonable. Unfortunately, the problem is that over the long term, more than 90 per cent of these 'actively managed funds' fail to even match the performance of the FTSE-100 index, the stock market average. There's plenty of evidence for that and here's just some of it:

1. Extracted from the *Investors Chronicle* on 22 March 1996:
   How few UK unit trusts (equity growth, growth and income, and income sectors) beat the market.

Value of £100 after...	1 yr	5yrs	10yrs
FTSE All-Share Index	£129	£200	£380
Average UK unit trust	£118	£169	£289
No. of unit trusts in existence	362	312	203
No. beating All-Share	16	25	15

The figures are from Micropal and show the value of £100 invested with dividends reinvested. UT returns are after costs and on an offer to bid basis.

The conclusion from these figures is that only 15 out of a total 203 UK unit trusts succeeded in beating the market average over ten years. That's just 7.4 per cent, leaving 92.6 per cent *under*performing.

2. According to Lipper, the research organization, only 16 out of 280 actively managed funds, or 5.7 per cent, beat the FTSE All-Share Index over the five years to the end of February 1999 when you take into account management charges. In other words over 94 per cent *failed to beat the index*.

3. A very extensive study, performed by the WM company, is displayed on the Web in its entirety at: **http://www.index-tracking.co.uk/**. The gems from this study are that:

• Over five years, 106 out of 114 unit trusts studied (93 per cent) *failed to beat the index* between 1994 and 1998, when you take into account charges and the inevitable cost of buying and selling shares, known as the bid-offer spread.

• Actively managed unit trusts were more volatile (i.e. their value swung more extremely), but the more volatile they were, the lower the returns. In other words, taking on extra risk and a more volatile strategy didn't pay off.

• Over the entire period of the study the probability of selecting a unit trust in the top quarter of performance based on historic top performance was no better than would be expected by chance. In other words, simply picking the actively managed unit trusts which have done well in the past doesn't work. You have to find the top performing managers *before* they have started to do well. Hmm.

Suppose, however, if we could find a fund that was pretty much guaranteed, over the long term, to come close to matching the index. Would we go for it? Well, if the charges were low enough, it would make sense, don't you think?

Such funds do, in fact, exist. They are called index trackers, and their only aim is to mirror the performance of a specific index. And you know what? These funds require no complicated company analysis and employ fewer highly-paid 'professionals', so their charges are generally much lower than those of actively managed funds too. Are they Foolish? We think so.

Don't forget, the UK stock market has managed an average return of around 12 per cent per year over the last eighty years, or over 8 per cent if you take inflation into account. Coming close to matching that would be a pretty good start on the road to Foolishness.

And which indexes can you track? The two most popular indexes to track in the UK are the FTSE-100 and the FTSE All-Share. The FTSE-100 represent the 100 largest companies on the London Stock Exchange. The FTSE All-Share includes the FTSE-100, but adds on the next 700 or so largest companies as well. As FTSE-100 companies make up approximately 80 per cent of the FTSE All-Share index by market capitalization anyway, there is likely to be relatively little difference, over the long term, between tracking any of the indices which include the top 100 UK companies.

But how do index trackers actually work?

In the case of the FTSE-100, for instance, all that is needed is to divide the total pot of money between all 100 companies, buying an amount of each company in proportion to its weighting in the FTSE-100 index. For example, the UK's largest company, BP Amoco, accounts for approximately 9.5 per cent of the FTSE-100, so 9.5 per cent of the total index tracker fund would be invested in BP Amoco shares. This method, known as full replication, should match the index exactly. In practice though, there will be some error, know as tracking error, and this is mainly due to the impracticality of adjusting the proportions of the various investments exactly as needed.

Many people would instinctively be attracted to a fund that outperforms the market. For a tracker fund though, outperformance is a failure, and may be a sign that the fund is not being managed as well as it should. One year's outperformance can easily become next year's underperformance, so when selecting a tracker fund, choosing the 'best performing tracker' is not what counts. Minimum tracking error, and low charges, are really the only meaningful measurements of a tracker fund's performance.

Full replication is not the only way to track an index. It is very difficult to apply to the All-Share index, for example, simply because of the large number of companies that make up that index. Spreading the fund that thinly would increase the cost of running the fund. Most funds that track the FTSE All-Share Index, therefore, use a system of tracking known as partial replication, in which the fund selects a smaller number of shares that are expected to be 'representative' of the index. There is a chance that a poorly representative selection of companies will be chosen, of course, so the tracking error for an All-Share tracker may be a little higher than for a FTSE-100 tracker. In reality, there's often not much difference and of course the All-Share is a much broader index to track. The final message: there is much less at stake in choosing between a FTSE-100 or FTSE All-Share tracker than between a tracker and an actively managed unit trust.

And how do you find the right tracker fund? There are three main things that you need to look for when making your choice:
1. Which index have you decided you want to track?
2. What are the charges? An annual charge of 1 per cent, with no initial or final charges, is the maximum we should ever pay for a tracker, though some trackers charge as little as 0.5 per cent per year.
3. What is the tracking error? The lower the better.

How do we find out this information? The Motley Fool Index Tracker message board contains a lot of discussion on, surprise, surprise, index trackers. Read on.

One Fool's Buying Decision

Often, trawling the Motley Fool message boards, you come across a bit of work done by a visiting Fool and posted for all to see that far surpasses what you, yourself, could achieve. Such a moment occurred today as I was planning out a section for this book on how to select an index tracker. I was about to rush off and search the Internet for the information, but first I thought I would check out our Index Tracker message board to see what Fools have been writing. Lo and behold, I find a message from Sean, who writes under the Motley Fool user name *mannalls*, which covers almost exactly what I wanted to write about.

Remember, most Fools posting on the message boards are just like you. They visit the Motley Fool because they enjoy it. They are not employees of the Motley Fool, although all employees of the Fool are indeed Fools themselves, but they do it because they are motivated to help others and share information and ideas.

If you want to read the original version of this message, which goes into a fair amount more detail and runs through Sean's reasoning a little more, type this long and complicated address into your browser: **http://boards.fool.co.uk/ Message.asp?id=2040010000253000&sort=id**. Better still, and far simpler, visit the Index Tracker message board and type message number '857' into the appropriate box and hit the return key. Then, as if by magic, you will find yourself swept over to Sean's original posting.

Here, then, in a somewhat abbreviated form, is the anatomy of one person's tracker buying decision:

WHICH INDEX TO TRACK?

The FTSE-100 has provided the best UK index returns recently, but over the long term, smaller companies can go through phases of performing better. If you believe that smaller companies are undervalued at the moment, you might want to look at a FTSE All-Share (FTSE-AS) tracker. The FTSE-AS is still 80 per cent by value made up of FTSE-100 companies though, so it isn't all high-risk stuff.

Mergers might eventually pose a problem for FTSE-100 trackers, as they may not have more than 10 per cent of the fund in any one company. BP Amoco makes up approx. 9 per cent of the FTSE-100, and could potentially breach the 10 per cent rule one day.

Tracking errors tend to be lower for FTSE-100 trackers, as they can easily buy all 100 companies proportionately. There are too many companies in the FTSE-AS though, so FTSE-AS trackers usually buy a representative sample of companies instead.

If you believe that medium-sized companies offer better value, tracking the FTSE-250 may make for a sensible investment, while a FTSE-350 tracker will give you a mix of both FTSE-100 and FTSE-250 companies.

There are lots of FTSE-100 trackers to choose from, and quite a few FTSE-AS trackers too. But for tracking either the FTSE-250 or FTSE-350, there is far less choice.

WHICH INDEX TRACKER PROVIDER TO USE?

Rule number one says: 'Never pay more than 1 per cent in annual charges, and never pay an up-front charge.' For the FTSE-100, there are many providers to choose from, including big names such as Virgin, M&S and Direct Line, all of whom charge around the 1 per cent mark. Scottish Widows currently charges only 0.5 per cent as standard, with a 0.25 per cent offer until April 2000.

For an All-Share tracker, the choice is more limited. Virgin charges 1 per cent. Fidelity and Legal & General are cheaper, with Fidelity charging 0.5 per cent and L&G 0.55 per cent. Legal & General are my preferred choice, though many Fools have praised Fidelity's telephone operatives and have criticized those at L&G (for trying to push non-Foolish products, for example).

Barclays b2 provides the only Foolishly priced FTSE-350 that I know of, with charges of 1 per cent per year, but I could find no FTSE-250 trackers with Foolish charges.

Other companies offer USA, European, and Asian Trackers, so you'll have to shop around if you want one of those.

WHY I CHOSE LEGAL AND GENERAL

I wanted the greater diversification of the All-Share Index, so it had to be Fidelity or L&G really. For me, L&G wins because I want to put a bit into a European tracker too, and the company allows you to split your contributions between both. You can also move funds between them at no charge.

USEFUL WEB SITES

*Legal & General (ISA page) – **http://www.landg.co.uk/ isa/isa1.html***
*Scottish Widows – **http://www.scottishwidows.co.uk***
*Fidelity – **http://www.fidelity.co.uk***
*Barclays b2 – **http://www.b2.com***
*Virgin – **http://www.virgin-direct.co.uk***
*AIB Govett – **http://www.aibgovett.com***
Foolish regards, Sean

Sean clearly lays out the reasons why he chose his particular fund, and you can see that he made his own choices. If you are a Fool, you will do the same yourself and choose an investment that suits your own requirements. Don't forget too, by the time you read this, charges may have changed from those quoted above and there may be a different range of trackers to choose from, so you will need to check for yourself.

At the time of writing, purchasing of funds such as index trackers over the Internet is still a bit sketchy. Although you can download some prospectuses from individual fund managers' Web sites, there is nowhere where you can go to buy one of a selection of different providers' funds. This is set to change, however, with the advent of fund 'supermarkets', which will allow you to buy and sell funds in a similar way to the way in which online brokers allow you to buy and sell shares. Keep an eye open for these springing up.

Chapter 6
Foolish Basics III: Investment Strategies at the Fool

Many of us wish to invest in individual shares, reckoning we can equal, if not beat the market average. And that's what most of the rest of this book is about. Here, we'll take a very brief overview of how you go about selecting which shares to buy. At points through the text, you'll find yourself directed to relevant parts of the Fool Web site, which look at the subjects in more detail and you'll also see the first of some screenshots of the Web site.

How do you select which shares to buy? It's a good question, and one to which, predictably, there is no firm answer, only some general thoughts and guidelines. Before we go on to those, though, let's make it clear once more that nothing you read here is a *recommendation* to buy, sell or do anything else. No, the ethos we try to develop at the Motley Fool is one of individual responsibility and education, so don't go looking for us to tell you what to do. You're on your own two feet and if you're happy with that idea, then read on. If not, go back.

The first thing to look at when prospecting for individual shares is your own life. Go on, stand back for a while! Survey the vista…

…

…

How's it looking?

A bit ugly, hey?

But we're not interested in the string of broken hearts, the dead-end job you should have chucked in years ago, or that cataclysmic moment when you broke wind on top of the vaulting horse, aged 12, to the hysterical merriment of the entire gym class (*and* the teacher). We're interested in what kind of products you use in your daily life, your leisure time, or the professional side of your existence. Chances are, you have some kind of specialist knowledge about one particular industry or group of products. Chances are, too, that at least some of the companies within that industry are 'listed' companies. That means that shares in those companies are listed on a stock exchange somewhere in the world. In Britain, that's likely to be on the London Stock Exchange, and it means you can become a part-owner in the company concerned; you can buy shares in it.

If you admire a company, you think it has good products, smart management and excellent prospects in a burgeoning industry, then that is a sound basis from which to start assessing it as an investment proposition.

Once you've picked over your daily life for investment prospects, widen the net by looking through the financial pages of the newspapers, in general interest magazines, chatting to friends or surfing the Web. You're sure to come up with something, likely a few well-known, major companies whose products and opportunities excite you.

Many people go on from this kind of approach to looking for shares of particular types. Some people specialize in one type, others seek to balance the style of their portfolio by investing in a few different types. We're not going to go into balancing your portfolio here, but just look at some of the different styles.

'Growth' investors look especially for booming companies in booming industries. They're after the small acorn which will grow into a massive oak tree in as short a time as possible. You'll find more on growth shares in general at the following section, which forms part of the stock ideas section at the Fool:

From **www.fool.co.uk**, click on 'Ideas' on the top tab bar.

'Value' investors, meanwhile, look particularly for shares which are undervalued because they are currently out of favour, but which are likely to bounce back. You'll find a series of highly entertaining thoughts on value investing by one of the Fool UK's greatest characters at the Value Investing area of our stock ideas section:

From **www.fool.co.uk**, click on 'Ideas' on the top tab bar.

The Qualiport is a real money portfolio at the Fool UK, which aims to buy outstanding companies at a reasonable price and hold them for the long-term. You can follow its progress, the reasoning behind its triumphs and its trials at:

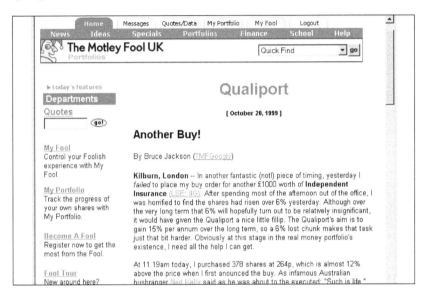

From **www.fool.co.uk**, click on 'Portfolios' on the top tab bar.

At the Motley Fool, we also find it helpful to think of companies in terms of 'Rule Makers' and 'Rule Breakers'. The first are companies which are dominant and set the rules of a particular industry, rules which other companies then have to follow. The second group, the Rule Breakers, tend to be smaller companies, which break the existing rules in total-ly unexpected ways and in so doing set up a new way of doing business. The capacity for growth with Rule Breakers, a kind of growth share, is generally higher, but not surpris-ingly they are much riskier.

Rule Making and Rule Breaking were two concepts first coined at the US Motley Fool and it's worth a visit to check out the two respective sites and the real-money portfolios fol-lowing the strategies:

Rule Makers

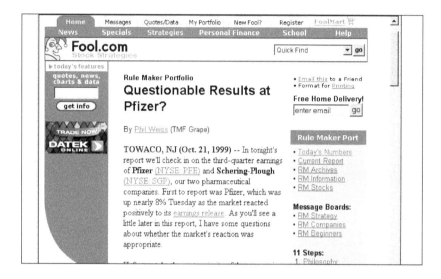

From **www.fool.com** click on 'Strategies' on the top tab bar.

Rule Breakers

From **www.fool.com** click on 'Strategies' on the top tab bar.

Not to be outdone, in the UK, we have the real money Rule Shaker portfolio, which seeks to embody the principles of both Rule Making and Rule Breaking and apply them outside the USA. Why 'Shaker'? Because it may be that those principles have to be shaken a little to work outside the USA. If you want to see how the British Fools are faring with respect to their US cousins, this is where you need to go:

From **www.fool.co.uk** click on 'Portfolios' on the top tab bar.

Finally, many people are attracted by mechanical investment strategies, which have proved their historical worth, both in the UK and the USA. These require discipline and an ultra long-term approach. As such they are deeply contrary and rather Foolish. Much work goes on at the UK Fool (and the US Fool) into developing and testing new mechanical strategies. Stop by the UK Foolish Workshop for an insight and to watch Fools beavering away:

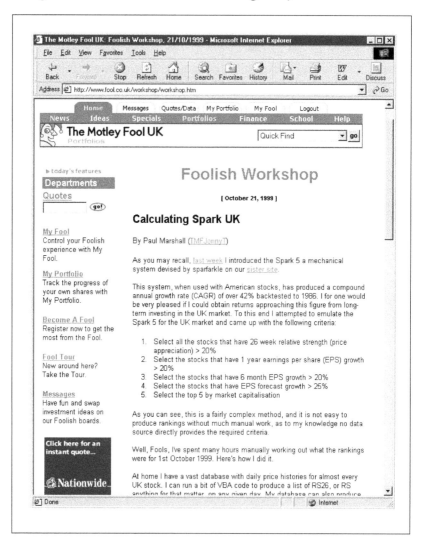

From **www.fool.co.uk** click on 'Portfolios' on the top tab bar.

To see some really crazy mechanical strategy fiends at work, stop by the US Motley Fool's Foolish Workshop:

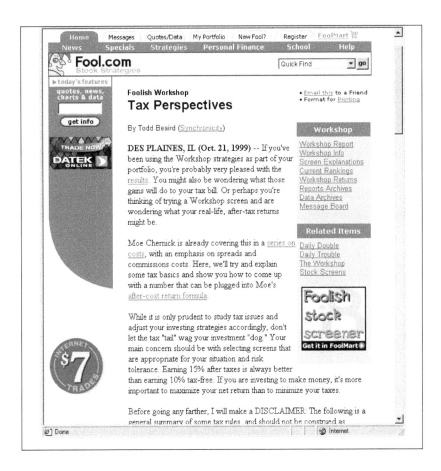

From **www.fool.com** click on 'Strategies' on the top tab bar.

In short, there are many ways to look at individual shares and everything you've read here is a taster. It sets the scene and lays out the territory, but doesn't fill in the gaps. If this is all you know about selecting individual shares, you don't yet know enough. There's a fair bit more to learn about shares, basic company financial information, investment strategies, potential pitfalls and what have you, before you go on to make your first investment. The next chapter, Eight Foolish Investing Guidelines, is an excellent place for some more ground rules.

Chapter 7
Foolish Basics IV: Eight Foolish Investing Guidelines

What follows are some investing guidelines for investing in individual shares which we have developed at the Motley Fool and which we think help make for a clear, low hassle, low stress approach to investing. We think they provide a solid foundation from which to build your long-term wealth. They're our opinion, of course, but we think you may find them helpful.

1. Don't Do Anything at All

One of the things we encourage at the Fool is to track the progress of a series of imaginary investments for a while before you even think of committing any hard cash to the process. That way, you get a feel for share price movements and can watch market swings with a tranquility and *sang froid* you may not otherwise have as a novice investor with real cash committed to the stock market. After a while, you start to realize that the market does move up and down a fair amount, and with it the prices of your shares. However, medium- to long-term – five years or more – the direction of the market has historically been upwards. Resoundingly so. There seems little reason why that should change.

How long should you not do anything at all? That's up to you. It may be three months, six months, a year or longer. Above all, don't rush in when you don't yet know enough, a fatal mistake. Only you can decide when the time is right.

2. Buy and Hold

Be a long-term Fool, buying and holding quality companies for the ultra long term, not one prey to the short-term vagaries of the market. Don't buy or sell shares in a company simply on the basis of their price alone. You're after long-term quality. If you believe the company is a good one, with sound positioning and terrific prospects, stand by those beliefs and continue to hold on to them if the share price happens to go down. If you're right, it will come up again in the future. Don't be scared into selling, just because everyone else is. Of course, if the situation in the company changes and there is *good reason* for a decline in the share price, that's an entirely different matter. Often, however, you'll find there isn't good reason and the shares are simply bouncing around a lot.

3. Avoid Penny Shares

Advertising in financial publications, you may see offers which look a bit like this:

GET RICH NOW!!! INSIDER OPPORTUNITY WITH PENNY SHARES!!

Firstly, anyone who has to SHOUT! to put their point across is already pretty suspect. Secondly, these are almost always advertisements for what are known as penny share tipsheets or newsletters. Penny shares are shares whose prices sit around the several pence range and in which the value of the company is generally just a few million pounds (which isn't much in the stock market scheme of things). Their share price is highly volatile, which means it shifts up and down a lot in percentage terms. Penny stock companies generally have very few shares in circulation, making it tough to sell them and when you do manage to, the spread between the buy and sell prices (the bid-offer spread) is generally very high. Also, there is often very little information available about the company in the public domain, meaning you have to base your decisions much more on hunches or guesswork.

Penny shares are far more likely to drop to zero than make you a packet, whatever investment tipsheets say. At the Motley Fool, we have set ourselves a limit which currently stands at a share price of 50p and/or a market capitalization of £30 million. If a company falls below this level on either count, we generally won't touch them.

Neither, we believe, should you.

4. No Share Tips
Whether they come from a newsletter, from a friend, or a rumour on the Internet, don't listen to share tips, especially those which allude to some kind of insider information. This is information which is known by someone on the inside and is not in the public domain. If it were, it would move the share price one way or the other. Acting on such information is called insider dealing and is illegal.

In any case, share tips on the basis of a rumour are almost always wrong. If you get your fingers burned as a result, you have only yourself to blame. Always invest on the basis of your *own* research and your *own* responsibly formed opinion. That can include chatting to other people about a company, either in person or on Internet message boards, but does not mean blindly acting on the basis of another's 'advice'.

5. Track Your Returns Against the Index
Few investment professionals do this, for the good reason that most of them fail to beat the market average, or the stock market index. You, however, shouldn't make this mistake. See how you do over time. If after a number of years you're consistently failing to beat what an index tracker would have brought in, think again. Maybe it's time for you to call it quits and consider shifting your funds over to a tracker.

If, on the other hand, you are hammering the index and your returns are soaring to the heavens over a period of years, then it's time for a little celebration, some well-deserved back-slapping and, who knows, maybe even enjoy a little holiday? Torquay's very pleasant in November, we hear. Go on, live a little!

6. Don't Invest in Too Many Shares. Or Too Few

Too few shares will mean that your portfolio will be prone to more extreme price fluctuations. Too many and you won't be able to keep track of them all. The right number is for you to decide, as is the type of companies you choose to invest in. Which are your favourites: more solid, more dependable companies, or more speculative Rule Breakers? The decision and the mix of the different types of shares can only be decided by you, but at the Fool we reckon on five to fifteen shares as being a good average holding for a portfolio. Some say five is too few, others fifteen is too much, so the range seems about right.

7. Don't Jump Off a Tall Building and Don't Time the Market

The market is going to tumble at some point in your investing career. It will, to lapse for one unwonted instant into the vernacular, 'go for a burton'. This must happen and with it an endless parade of talking heads will appear on TV, predicting disaster, hell fire and brimstone. The press will become obsessed that the Crash of 1929 is in the process of being repeated. Meanwhile, the value of your portfolio will have gone down 10, 20, 30, even 40 per cent and your pacing has speeded up, wearing down a furrow in the dining room floor which deepens with every passing hour.

It's scary, all right. But we urge you not to jump off a tall building or do anything else precipitate. Think carefully before you sell all your shares, because if you're unlucky it may *not* be the end of the world.

During the four trading days from 29 September 1998 to 5 October 1998, the FTSE-100 index screamed down 9 per cent. Youch! Would you have been tempted to sell? Who wouldn't? The newspapers were certainly full of doom and gloom and 'end of the world is nigh' stuff.

Well, that could have been a big mistake because in the five trading days from 5 October 1998 to 12 October 1998, the FTSE-100 rose a surprising 8.4 per cent[4]. How many people, breathing a sigh of relief at avoiding calamity in that first week, would have had the clairvoyance or the foresight to buy back in for the second week? Very, very few, we'll wager. They'd have missed out on recouping their 'paper' losses and would have been sitting on a real loss instead.

Try and stay cool and understand that despite short-term swings, the *long-term* direction of the market has always been upwards. Market timing is a hard, perhaps impossible, art to master. We steer clear of it.

8. Share Your Knowledge With Others

Finally, let's end on an uplifting note. Knowing what you know now and are likely to learn in the future puts you into a small, select group of people. Few of us know much about money, meaning that those who do have the capacity for great good if they choose to share it for the benefit of others. The knowledge and understanding you are putting together is something valuable. It's a jewel. Don't keep it to yourself. Instead, dispel some of the ignorance and fear surrounding this most vital subject by sharing it about.

End of the Basics

But that's all it is. The basics. From here on in, we'll be talking mainly about the mechanics of the Internet and how to use it for investing. For more on investing strategies and the like you'll have to visit our Web site or read our other books.

Before we move on, though, here's a vital thought to hang onto for the rest of your journey:

Online investing is magically convenient and opens up many possibilities, but that doesn't change any of the basic ground rules of good investing sense. Always make sure you do justice to yourself by ensuring you have a sound grasp and understanding of what you're doing. And always maintain a long-term focus.

---

[4] Actual data, as derived from Motley Fool archives: FTSE-100 close on 29 September 1998 – 5108.7; on 5 October 1998 – 4648.7; on 12 October 1998 – 5037.6.

Chapter 8
Why use the Internet for Investing?

There are three main reasons for using the Internet to help with investing:

Firstly it is an invaluable source of information.

Secondly it enables you to communicate with thousands of other investors.

Thirdly it enables you to take control of your own financial destiny.

Let's run through them, one by one, in the excruciating, aching and mind-numbingly tedious detail you have now come to expect from the Motley Fool:

[*Hey! Who put that in there?*]

Information

Not so long ago the private investor was at a major disadvantage compared to those very important and very well-paid Wise men (for mostly they are) in suits working in the City of London. We had little access to information, and what we could get was almost always out of date. If we did want information, we had to pay for it and pay pretty heavily.

The Internet has changed all of that. Now the private investor has access to an enormous amount of information and what's more, increasingly information on the Internet is free. Even just a year or two ago, you had to pay often hefty subscriptions for what today comes free. This is an unstoppable trend and at the Fool we're excited to see that continue. We see the increasing thirst for high quality, free information as one of the major driving forces behind the Internet.

In Chapter 9, we'll take a step-by-step walk through the different types of information readily available on the Web. We will see how we can gain an amazing amount of data about any company which interests us.

What about information overload? Is that a real worry? We don't think so and we also think that this is simply another thing for the media to present as something to worry about. After all, it's things for people to worry about that sell newspapers. No, as we see it, the capacity to deal with, filter and classify information is increasing in parallel with the amounts of information becoming available. That increasing capacity is to be found on the Web itself, where sites increasingly recognize the need to package and present information in digestible, useful forms. It's also to be found within ourselves. We're just getting better at figuring out what is important and shutting off to things which aren't. Like any other skill, it's a question of practice.

At the end of this Foolish Guide, you'll find a list of links to sources for all types of investment-related information. Some of the links will help you find out all the information you need on a particular company, others will provide more general guidance. Some you'll find exceedingly helpful, others less so. It's a question of trying them out and finding which sites present the information you want in the way that you want it to be presented. And if you can't find a site which tells you exactly what you want, why not start your own? Who knows? You may have just identified a niche business opportunity on the Web which will turn you into an Internet tycoon. Stranger things have happened. Far, far stranger.

Communication
Over at the US Motley Fool, Rob Landley (Motley Fool screen name: TMF Oak) wrote an article in 1999 on the nature of the Internet, which makes interesting reading. He wrote:

'The spread of the Internet around the globe was not driven by companies selling their wares through web pages. At first it was driven by e-mail, then newsgroups, and finally a web of personal home pages. And one of those personal home pages was called Yahoo!'

He points out that Yahoo! wasn't started to make money, but to provide a service. Two college students wanted to find fun things on the Web, but there was no organization to the thousands of personal home pages which then existed, except for links from one page to another. So, they explored this new realm themselves and kept a list of pages that they liked. Almost as an afterthought, they put that list up on their own Web page, and that's where the real fun began. That index of sites became a popular destination, and other surfers who used it contributed the results of their own explorations, making Yahoo! all the more valuable. The new dynamic put the power of publication and peer review – the driving force of science – into the hands of individuals everywhere. As more people used the resource, more suggestions for improvement and corrections of mistakes trickled in, and the value of Yahoo! to its users grew. Volunteers were needed to maintain it, but why not if it was fun and useful and not too much work? Since then, of course, Yahoo! has mushroomed into one of the leading world-wide Internet brands.

Rob noted that the real power of the Internet lies in the potential for collaboration. Certainly, the Motley Fool carries articles written by staff members with a 'TMF' screen name like Rob's, but in reality the success of the Fool is based on the successful collaboration of users sharing investment information and ideas. The analysis you'll find there – to which anyone in the entire population is free to contribute, remember – is often far more penetrating than what comes out of Wall Street or the City of London. Largely, that's because the reasoning often comes from users of a particular company's products or people with particular experience of that industry themselves. That reasoning is also published openly and laid bare for others to read and comment on;

nothing is hidden. Fools will quickly point out errors and mistakes in each other's thinking, generally in a constructive and pretty harmonious way. For anyone who takes a sour view of human nature, or thinks the Internet robs us of true human experience, the Motley Fool's message boards would be an eye-opener. Here's the link to Rob's article:

http://www.fool.com/portfolios/rulemaker/1999/rule maker990611.htm

I believe I have learnt more about investing over the last two years of working with the Motley Fool through the interactions I have had on the message boards than I did in the previous ten years of reading about it and also actively investing in the stock market. Working alone, I did 'so-so'. But being able to share my ideas, being told I had got it wrong, and then being able to blatantly pinch other peoples' ideas have improved my own thinking and have transformed the way I invest.

And now it's time to introduce Deep Blue. Deep Blue? Yes, you may remember that in 1997 a computer of that name, designed and programmed by IBM to play chess, managed to beat Gary Kasparov, the world chess champion. This was a remarkable event, and was the first time that a computer had been able to beat the best human chess mind. Immediately afterwards we all saw the breathless newspaper headlines: MACHINE BEATS MAN! Was that fair? You judge after you've read what comes next. You see, Gary Kasparov was not really beaten by a machine. He was beaten by a team of many highly skilled computer programmers, backed by the stupendous resources of IBM and a legion of chess analysts, who designed an algorithm that was based on thousands (no millions) of games played between humans. It was able to select winning traits, and used the number crunching power of the computer to develop a game strategy that was good enough, and flexible enough, to beat the great-est chess grand master we have ever seen.

No, a machine did not beat Gary Kasparov. He was ultimately beaten by the collective abilities of thousands of people. All the machine did was serve as a conduit by which that collective expertise could be channelled and focused. For more on the Deep Blue story, this is where you want to go:

http://www.research.ibm.com/deepblue/home/html/b.html

With appropriate humility and due respect for the phenomenal achievement of Deep Blue, we like to view the Motley Fool and its message boards as being just a little similar to it. By acting as a conduit, the message boards allow the collective expertise and intelligence of thousands of people to manifest in a way which would have been impossible prior to the Internet. Therein is much of the true value of what the Fool offers.

What is perhaps most extraordinary about the whole thing is the way in which each message posted adds so much to the entire phenomenon: the more contributions there are, the more valuable the whole thing becomes. But it's not a straight line graph, rather it's one of those fancy exponential curves. In other words, the value increases more and more rapidly all the time. Imagine the power 20,000, 2,000, 200, or even 20 investors interested in a particular company can have if they put their collective thoughts together. This is what is happening right now, here at the Fool. If you log into the message boards, you will find a myriad of conversations going on all the time, about all kinds of things money-related and many things which are not.

In Chapter 13 on Getting the Best Out of the Fool, we take a more in-depth look at the Motley Fool message boards and how to use them to best effect.

Taking Control

By making available to you a huge amount of information and the reflective power of many thousands of other investors, the Internet allows you to take complete control of your financial destiny and assume responsibility for your investment decisions. As we've seen, these are exceedingly powerful tools. Focused correctly and sorted efficiently (and the Fool is here to help you do just that), they will put you in a position of unprecedented power. What that power means to you is this:

• Saving money on pointless financial advice from professional advisers.

• Earning greater returns than you would have by following that potentially harmful advice.

• Basking in a sense of well-being and ease, knowing that you have your financial future securely in hand and that you are Captain of your Fate and Master of your Soul.

All this is yours for the taking and entirely thanks to the Internet. It means freedom, it means independence, it means money becomes an area of your life that is fulfilling and enriching (forgive the pun), instead of a drag. It's no wonder that we're a bit freakily overenthusiastic about it at times. You will be too when you've experienced it for yourself.

Chapter 9
Researching Individual Companies

Now we're starting to get down to what the Internet can actually offer you. No more waffly stuff, here is where we turn into mean, serious and hungry Internet investors. Let's presume you have heard about a company and you are interested in it as a potential investment. You may have read about it in a newspaper and become fascinated, you may be a regular user of its products, you may have first heard about it at the Fool, or perhaps its name was spelled out at one of your regular Thursday night Ouija board sessions. Whatever. You want to know more. How are you going to go about it?

The first thing is to figure out what kinds of things you would want to know about a potential investment anyway. Then we'll have a look and see where we can find this stuff on the Web. Throw us a few suggestions and we'll 'yea' or 'nay' them as appropriate. Ready, here we go!

What exactly their business is.
Yea!

How much money they make.
Yea!

How their share price has performed in the past few years.
Yea!

What other investors think of them.
Yea!

Their annual report.

Yea!

How big they are.
Yea!

How much money City analysts think they'll make in the future.
Yea!

Any major items of recent news about them.
Yea!

Information about the directors which you might be able to use to blackmail them.
Nay, nay, a thousand times, na-a-ay!

You're getting the wrong idea here. The Fool stands for wholesome entertainment for all the family. We don't do things like that. Back on message and try again.

Whether the directors have recently been buying or selling shares in their own company.
Better, much better. Yea!

All this stuff is easily accessible on the Internet for most of the companies you're likely to be interested in. And it's all free. Just a few years ago, you wouldn't have had a chance of assembling all this information without paying a hefty sum for it and even then it would have taken days, if not weeks, to put together. Some of it wasn't available at all.

Now, which company are we going to use as an example? Well, we're going to presume Edwin, the office nerd, knobbled you at the coffee machine at 11 o'clock this morning:

'I'm telling you Arm occupies a cornerstone position in the mobile market. They're not just box-shifters, they design the chips for 75 per cent of the world's mobile phones and if the Symbian venture comes off, which I frankly think it will, it's hard to see where the opportunity stops. Hot chocolate or cappuccino?'

Edwin's always talking about his latest favourite technology company and although you gave him the brush-off and mocked him gently, secretly you're a little bit interested. Edwin's a pretty bright bloke and always manages to fix your computer when it breaks down. And your car! Maybe he knows what he's talking about. You sit down at your screen, ready to employ the awesome resources of the Internet to see if this is all just Edwin-speak or if there's really something in it. A supernatural force takes over (it's eerie) and guides your hand, causing you, as if by magic, to type the letters **http://www.fool.co.uk** into your browser and hit the 'Enter' key. Up pops the Motley Fool home page, where you spy the tab at the top of the page which says 'Quotes and Data'.

You hit the Quotes and Data tab and get taken to this page:

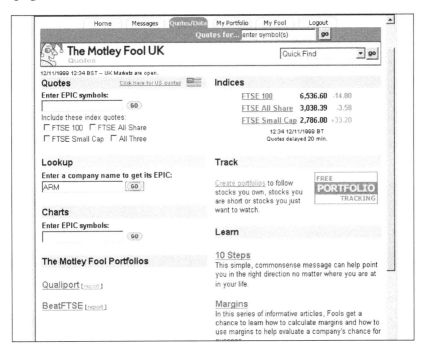

Warp speed changes on the Internet and in particular at the Fool mean that by the time you read this, the Quotes and Data page will likely have changed a little, but it will be broadly recognizable. Anyway, you want information about ARM. To get that, you will have to enter ARM's EPIC symbol. (Before you say 'Whaaaat?!' we explain EPICs on page 122.) The problem is you don't know what ARM's EPIC is. You could try guessing it (hint: it's pretty obvious), or you could try looking it up. You decide to look it up, which you do by entering 'ARM' in the small field where it says 'Lookup' and then hitting 'Go'. This takes you to:

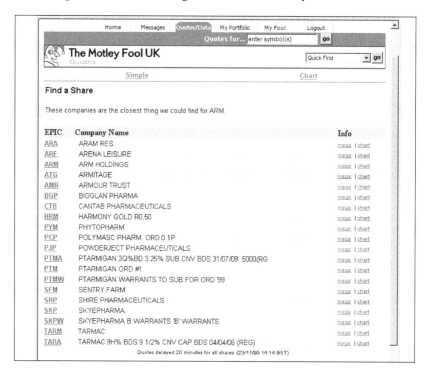

You can see that the only company which matches is a company called 'Arm Holdings'. You're getting warm! You click on the highlighted 'ARM' EPIC symbol (we told you it was obvious) on the left side of the screen and, hey presto, you're transported to this page:

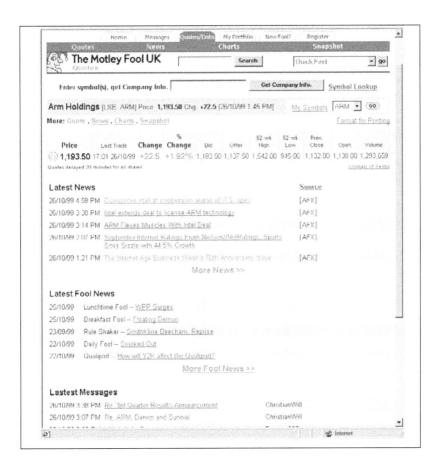

Or at least to somewhere very similar to this page. Warp speed changes on the Internet – blah, blah, blah – mean that this mockup of how the Fool's data offering will appear may have been superceded by the time you look at it. It will contain all the same elements, but perhaps organized in a slightly snazzier manner. No matter, the data is here; what have we got?

Going through it in a logical order, we can see that the company is called Arm Holdings and the 'LSE: ARM' in brackets next to it means it is traded on the London Stock Exchange (LSE). We can see the most recent price it traded at (actually 20 minutes delayed), which in this case is 1,193.50. We can also see that its 52-week high price has been 1,542.00 and its 52-week low price has been 945.00, a difference of 39 per cent. This is a share whose price doesn't stay still for long. At this point, we're idly wondering if the last year has seen a steady rise, or a roller-coaster journey. Well, just below the price information, you can see links to 'More'. That offers you 'News', 'Charts' or 'Snapshot'. Hit 'Charts'. That will take you to a page like this:

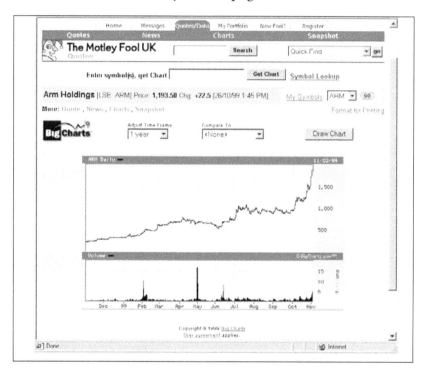

This is a chart of the share price of ARM for the last year. Although it's been a bumpy ride at times, the rise has been pretty inexorable and frankly phenomenal. Something interesting has been happening here. Maybe Edwin was right. If we wish, we can also choose to view the share price over a longer period and can see how it has done as compared to the FTSE All-Share, FTSE-100 or the FTSE Small Cap share indices.

Happy with the charts? They're a great way of portraying a company's share price performance and tell you broadly whether the market loves or hates the share. Hit the back button again.

We'll talk about news very shortly, but for the moment we want to look at the company snapshot, so do us a favour and click on that now, will you?

Thanks. This gives you contact details for the company and a one line summary of its activities. We now know it's a micro-processor marketing, research and development company. Worth knowing. Below that description are three years' worth of summary financial information. At this point, you may or may not be interested in that. If you're someone who digests numbers like a mid-morning snack, then have a read through; otherwise hit the back button on your browser once more.

Now, it's time to turn our attention to the news. Scanning down the page, we see that there are two sets of headlines. There are the 'Latest headlines' and the 'Latest Fool Headlines'. In the live version, the 'Latest Headlines' will be the latest headlines from the AFX news agency relating to ARM. The 'Latest Fool Headlines' are, of course, the latest headlines from the Motley Fool Globalwire news agency and hot dog stand, relating to ARM.

Having a scan through some of these will give you a feel for what's been in the news for ARM recently. If you want more detail, click through where it says 'More Headlines'. That will take you through to the next ten headlines in chronological order.

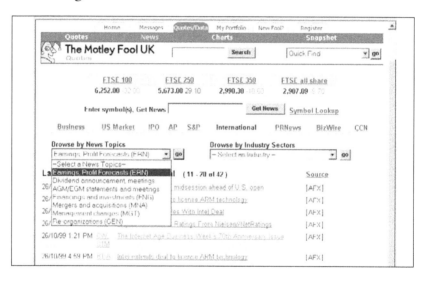

But there's more. As you can see, that page also has a drop-down menu which allows you to view historical news items classified according to:
1. Earnings, profit forecasts
2. Dividend announcements, meetings
3. AGM/EGM statements and meetings
4. Financing and investments
5. Mergers and acquisitions
6. Management changes
7. Reorganizations

If all this news is starting to look a bit daunting, let's remember we're here trying to get a feel for this company and don't want to run through absolutely everything. What is most going to interest us at this point are items 1 and 3. The earnings results and profit forecasts will tell us how well the company has been performing recently and how well City analysts think it will perform in the future. The Annual General Meeting statements will give us some kind of round up of the company's view of the preceding year.

Having milked the news agency news for all it's worth, let's pop back to the main ARM data page and check out some of the Fool headlines. One of the ones we find from 18 October 1999 refers to the Daily Fool of that day. The Fool's Eye View section of that daily piece, which is a longer article looking at a particular subject in more depth, is all about Arm. It's written by Stuart Watson, staff writer at the Motley Fool, who lives life under the rather grand user name, 'TMF Tiger' (he isn't really, he's a pussycat):

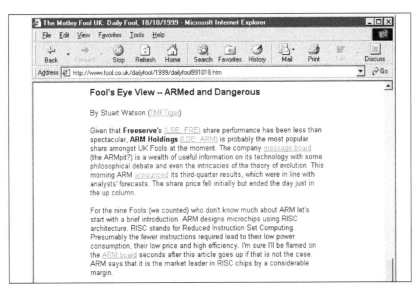

Now you know all kinds of interesting things about ARM, including that it designs microchips using the RISC architecture, which stands for 'Reduced Instruction Set Computing'. You also know that their main source of income comes from licensing their chip design out to manufacturers, that their profit margins are good for a small technology company and a whole lot more. You'll have something to tell Edwin when you next see him. After checking out a couple more Fool headlines, you zap back to the main ARM data page.

What now? Let's see what other Fools are thinking. At the bottom of the page we can see the latest five messages posted on the ARM message board at the Fool. Clicking on any one of those will take us directly into the message itself. Clicking on 'More messages' takes us to the board:

Home	Messages	Quotes/Data	My Portfolio	My Fool	Logout
Folders	Best of	Favourites / Replies	Customise		Help

The Motley Fool UK
Boards

Quick Find ▾ go

Shares A / Arm Holdings (ARM) quote

Post New   ◀SKIP 7 Days ▾ SKIP▶   Prev • Next

UnThreaded • Threaded	Author	Recs	Date	Number
Re: Investor of the Year	TMFTiger	--	26/10/99 09:49	974
Upgrade	TerryMcC	1	25/10/99 19:56	965
Purchase of ARM	khad29	--	25/10/99 23:38	971
Re: Purchase of ARM	licence	--	25/10/99 23:54	972
Re: Purchase of ARM	Foolest	1	26/10/99 01:06	973
Re: Purchase of ARM	tsh2	--	26/10/99 10:09	975
Re: Purchase of ARM	mipper	2	26/10/99 12:51	977
Re: Purchase of ARM	tsh2	--	26/10/99 13:00	978
Re: Purchase of ARM	aparsa	--	26/10/99 13:32	979
Re: Purchase of ARM	gollyevans	--	26/10/99 20:55	985
Re: Purchase of ARM	earsb	--	26/10/99 21:36	986
Re: Purchase of ARM	Foolest	--	26/10/99 23:08	987
Re: Purchase of ARM	JT355	--	26/10/99 23:31	988
Re: Purchase of ARM	Bullet10	--	26/10/99 23:43	989
Re: Purchase of ARM	angussb	--	27/10/99 03:22	991

As we can see, there's been a fair amount of discussion about this company. Flicking back through the board (don't worry – we go into how to use the boards in more detail in Chapter 13), we see some interesting threads of discussion. Let's pick one thread out and have a look. And the fickle finger of fate falls on, 'How will ARM get 70 per cent growth year after year?':

The Motley Fool UK
Boards

Quick Find ▼ go

Shares A / **Arm Holdings** (ARM) quote

Post New   ♥ ◀SKIP 7 Days ▼ SKIP▶   Prev • Next

UnThreaded • Threaded	Author	Recs	Date	Number
How will ARM get 70% growth year after year?	DiamondEdge	1	24/10/99 00:47	934
Re: How will ARM get 70% growth year after year?	Miten	2	25/10/99 10:52	945
Re: How will ARM get 70% growth year after year?	nmaitland	1	25/10/99 10:58	946
Re: How will ARM get 70% growth year after year?	dwinson	1	25/10/99 11:10	947
Re: How will ARM get 70% growth year after year?	urpo	1	25/10/99 11:44	948
Re: How will ARM get 70% growth year after year?	nmaitland	1	25/10/99 11:49	949
reason for Recent Recent price rise....	urpo	1	25/10/99 09:34	940
Latest announcement (Intel)	TMFTiger	1	25/10/99 09:57	941
Off Topic - Radstone Technology	TheCornishman	1	25/10/99 13:20	951
Rocket Ships	PrinceofGilts	1	25/10/99 15:09	954
Reuters summary of 25th Oct	PrinceofGilts	1	25/10/99 15:31	955
ARM & Intel	llamedos	--	25/10/99 15:47	956
Re: ARM & Intel	metamorphosis	--	25/10/99 22:24	969
Investor of the Year	TheCornishman	1	25/10/99 16:32	959
Re: Investor of the Year	stevedeer	--	25/10/99 16:38	960
Re: Investor of the Year	ptoboley	1	25/10/99 16:44	961
Re: Investor of the Year	TheCornishman	1	25/10/99 16:49	962
Re: Investor of the Year	TMFTiger	1	25/10/99 17:29	963
Re: Investor of the Year	TheCornishman	1	25/10/99 17:31	964

The thread starts with a question from a character called DiamondEdge:

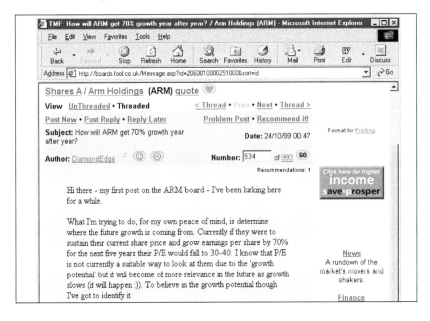

He gets answered by Miten and that seems pretty helpful:

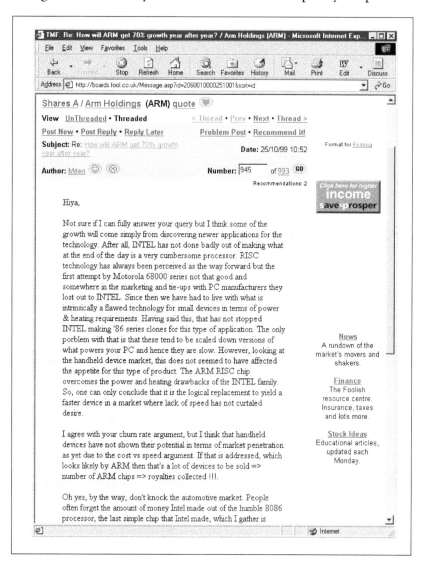

nmaitland jumps in next:

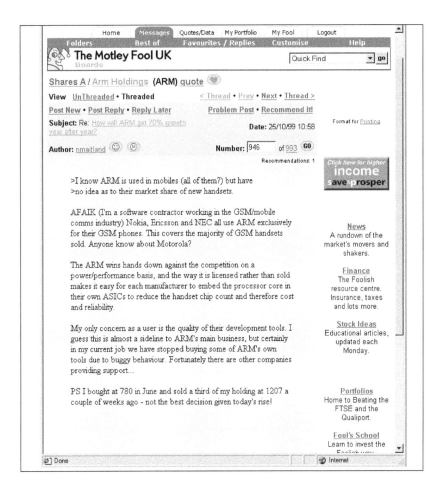

And so it goes on. Read a couple of threads like this and you're starting to get a feel for which are the big issues concerning investors in ARM.

Now it's time to see what ARM has to say for itself. We don't know the Web site address, so we try a couple of likely ones on spec. First, we type in **http://www.arm.co.uk**. Oops! That takes us to a company which is called ARM, but isn't the ARM we're looking for at all. They must have nabbed the address first. Nice move! Next, we try **http://www.arm.com.** That's it:

Quite a busy, overcrowded front page, but we like the look of all those logos, signifying their partnership deals. At this point, we'll probably spend a while surfing round their site, seeing what they have to say about their products and getting a bit more of a feel for what the company is about. Fairly soon, we get to this page:

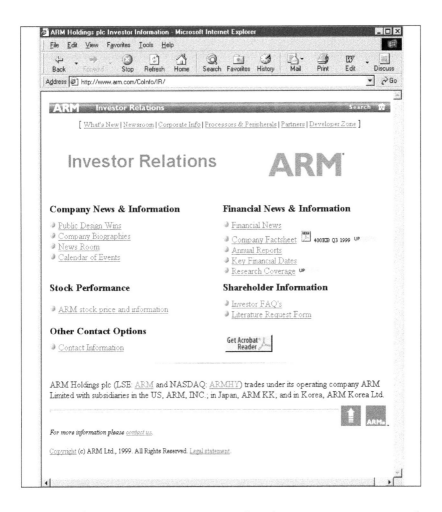

This is what we want! Company factsheet, company annual reports, investor FAQs (Frequently Asked Questions) and more. We have the *Adobe Acrobat Reader* program on our computer (if we don't, we download it) and therefore go ahead and download all the documents we're interested in *Acrobat* format, also known as 'pdf'. This basically means they will be readable as well-designed, well-presented documents, looking a bit like a magazine. That's a lot more pleasant to read than simply text. Once we've downloaded them, we open them up. This is what the front page of the Company Factsheet looks like:

NASDAQ - ARMHY
LSE - ARM
www.arm.com

ARM Holdings plc
Investor Fact Sheet
Q3 Update 1999

Silicon Partners

Include: 3COM, Alcatel, AKM, Atmel, Cirrus Logic, Conexant, Fujitsu, Hewlett Packard, Hyundai, IBM, Intel, LSI Logic, Lucent Technologies, Matsushita, Mitel, National Semiconductor, NEC, OKI, Philips, Qualcomm, Rohm, Samsung, Seiko Epson, Sharp, Sony, ST Microelectronics, Texas Instruments, Toshiba and Yamaha.

Software Partners

Include: ISI, Microsoft, Mentor Graphics, WindRiver, Sun Microsystems, and Symbian.

EDA and Tools Partners

Include: Cadence, CoWare, Hewlett Packard, IKOS, Lauterbach, Mentor Graphics, Synopsys, Tektronix, Yokogawa

Design Partners

Include: Cadence, Palmchip, Sirius Communications, Teknema, Wipro

Target Applications

Embedded Control
Automotive, Security, Mass Storage, Modems, Printers

Digital Consumer
Digital Cameras, Digital TV, Game Machines, GPS Systems, Set-Top-Boxes

Portable Products
Handheld PC's, Mobile Phones, PDA's, Smart Phones

OEM's Endorsing the ARM® Architecture

Embedded Control
Include: 3COM, Aristocrat, Gemplus, HP, Canadian Marconi, Cirrus, Rockwell, Virata

Digital Consumer
Include: Daewoo, Nokia, RCA, GI, Thomson, Samsung, Sharp, Sony

Portable Products
Include: Ericsson, Nokia, Panasonic Psion, Hagenuk, Siemens, Philips

CORPORATE OVERVIEW

ARM is a leading intellectual property (IP) provider that licenses high performance, low-cost, power-efficient microprocessors and system chips to international electronics companies for use in an extensive range of applications. ARM also sells software and development systems and provides consulting, support, maintenance and training services, to accelerate the acceptance of its architecture and products.

The company has created a growing global network of partners, which includes many of the leading semiconductor, software, design tool, EDA (Electronic Design Automation) and systems companies worldwide. ARM's semiconductor partners design, manufacture, market and sell microprocessors, application specific integrated circuits (ASICs) and application specific standard products (ASSPs) using ARM's standards. Adding their own technologies and capabilities the partners create differentiated products which capitalize on ARM's broadly supported open global standard architecture.

COMPANY HISTORY

The Company was established in Nov 1990 as a joint venture between Acorn, Apple and VLSI.

The ARM® architecture was the first RISC architecture designed for a low cost budget. Competing architectures originally focused on maximizing performance and were first used in workstations.

ARM Holdings plc was first listed on the London Stock Exchange (ARM) and Nasdaq (ARMHY) in April 1998. The original shareholders today own around 7.9% of the shares and in addition ARM employees also own approximately 7% of the Company (all employees are offered stock options). In April 1999, the shareholders of ARM Holdings plc approved a four for one stock split at its Annual General Meeting.

MISSION

ARM's mission is to establish its architecture as the standard for embedded RISC processors for use in a wide range of high volume applications, in the embedded, portable and consumer multimedia markets.

Examples of Products using ARM® Processors

This we print out to read on the tube on the way home. (You've been doing all this in your lunch break while munching your sandwiches, OK? You haven't been cyber-skiving, have you?)

Please note, we're not going to go too far into how you actually assess a company's accounts or the details of what you might be looking for in a company, as we don't have the space for it. That is dealt with sumptuously, commodiously, extravagantly, even, in the Motley Fool's other recently published tome, *The Motley Fool UK Investment Workbook* and, of course, at the Web site.

Already, we have access to a whole lot of information about ARM, but we're not quite finished yet. We might want to know whether the directors of the company are buying or selling shares in it. If they're buying shares, then that suggests they think the company is good value at the moment. If they're selling shares, on the other hand, does that mean they therefore think it's a bad investment and investors would be wise to steer clear? Not necessarily. Not necessarily at all. It could just mean that daughter Miranda needs a new pony for the gymkhana this year or that kitchen extension is costing more than the family first thought. The other thing we want to know is what the City analysts are forecasting upcoming profits to be. This is worth knowing because they receive regular private briefings from the company on how things are going (we think all those briefings should be made entirely public and on the record, by the way) and so are usually pretty on target with their estimates.

Both these sources of information are available at a number of places on the Internet and will almost certainly be available at the Fool by the time you read this.

We've really got a lot of information now, from a variety of different sources and are starting to build up a picture of ARM in our mind. This isn't a one-off process, though, after which you're done. Learning about and assessing companies as potential investment prospects is an ongoing adventure, with gaps to be filled in, new insights to be absorbed and, eventually, new insights for you to offer to others. As you learn more about the company, too, you'll want to check out its competitors to see if they may be better prospects or represent a significant threat. As you do this, you are building up a corpus of knowledge and experience which will give you increasing amounts of confidence.

You will find one of the most effective resources is likely to be the company message boards at the Motley Fool. Spend a little while going through old messages and get a feel for what the tenor of the board has been. You'll soon know who have been the major and who the minor contributors, who holds what opinion about the company and what the community believes the most important issues are. Mostly, you'll find the message boards live up to the ideal of 'constructive and open debate' which we champion here at the Fool and are a pleasant place to hang out. If there's some aspect of the company you can't get straight or are wondering about, by all means feel free to jump in and post the question. You'll almost certainly get a helpful response. Eventually, you might find yourself posting more and more, itching to get in there and respond to thoughts from one of the old lags which you happen to disagree with, or help out a newcomer with their questions.

Now, let's wind the calendar forward a week, perhaps two. It's once more 11 o'clock in the morning; you're feeling ropy. It's been a rough morning and you need caffeine. Bad. Back at the coffee machine, you meet Edwin. He's about to open his mouth and shoot you a stream of technobabble he thinks you won't understand when you say this (exactly this, memorize it):

'Yes, ARM are definitely interesting. I was particularly excited by the announcement of the licensing deal with Intel. Intel are going to base their StrongARM chips on the ARM 5TE chip, which has various enhancements. Intel's next StrongARMs will run at 150-600MHz, delivering 185-750 MIPS while consuming 40-450 milliwatts. They will implement seven-stage integer and eight-stage memory pipelines to achieve high execution rates at fast clock speeds, and use dynamic branch prediction and extensive data bypassing to increase data throughput. Nifty, hey? Cappuccino or hot chocolate, old man?'

Really, you don't have to go into that level of techno-detail to decide whether you want to invest in ARM or not, but it's worth faking it occasionally to watch the expression on Edwin's face.

Now, who said investing wasn't fun?

Chapter 10
Selecting an Online Broker

Right at the start, let's get one thing clear: opening a brokerage account is as easy as opening a bank account. Easier, even. There's no mystique to it. Anyone can do it. Because the idea of buying and selling shares directly through an online broker is a pretty new one in the UK, it's easy for us to be intimidated by the idea of having our own brokerage account. Many of us feel as if it's something for other people, people with more experience. That's wrong. Times have changed and now you can do it. You may want a little help at times, but that's why you're reading this book and why the Motley Fool site exists.

American investors have been enjoying cheap online brokerage services for quite some time, but online brokers are only now coming to prominence in Britain. That said, there are new ones opening up all the time, the growth is extraordinarily rapid and we can expect to see competition hotting up and prices coming down. As with all consumer products and services, growth in the market and the competition which that attracts are good for Foolish investors.

The Three Types of Broker

Before we look at trading shares online and at Internet brokers themselves, let's digress briefly and have a look at the different ways in which stockbrokers operate. There has always been a range of services available, with a range of charges to match.

The most comprehensive services (and the highest charges, of course) come from full service brokers. These learned and professional fellows will take control of all your cash for you and will manage your investments without you having to lift a finger. They will make all the decisions, buying and selling what they think best, and as often as they see fit. For that, they will charge you a fairly hefty commission, which usually takes the form of a percentage of every trade that they make on your behalf, along with a yearly portfolio management fee. They must know what they are doing though, mustn't they? They couldn't command such high fees if they weren't able to make you wealthy, could they? Well, actually, we just don't know. We have yet to hear of a full service broker who publishes the returns they have made for their clients as compared to the stock market index. If they're anything like their brethren who manage unit trusts, though, the vast majority probably underperform the index over time. If you do decide you need the services of such a broker, you'll probably need upwards of £100,000 to invest before they'll deem you worthy of gracing their establishments.

Who's Next?

Next step down the price ladder is to pay for advisory services only. Your broker still takes a commission from every trade you make, but only offers advice, rather than handling the whole thing for you. It's you who must make the final decision every time. Such a service is still expensive, still suffers from your broker's likely inability to beat the index in the long run, and still runs up against the classic conflict of interest which taints any middle man. Given the choice of recommending that you sell one share and buy another, which means a commission from both trades, or recommending that you stay put, which means no commission at all, we bet many advisory brokers will be tempted by Mammon. They're only human, after all.

Next!

Execution-only brokers. They sound deadly, but they're not. These brokers will carry out your orders for you, buying and selling exactly what you say, without offering any comment or advice whatsoever. As they don't do any investment management for you, and don't offer any advice, they don't do any investment research and don't have to employ expensive 'experts'. They can, therefore, charge a much lower sum for their services.

There are a whole variety of execution-only brokers, some offering postal and telephone services and increasing numbers offering real-time Internet dealing. These are the online brokers and are primarily what we're concerned with here.

Choosing Your Broker

With the number of execution-only brokers available, and the different flavours of service they offer, it is important to pick the right one, and the rest of this section is aimed at helping you to decide which is best for you. The information here is just a snapshot of the way things were at the time of writing, but it is also kept up to date on the Motley Fool site. Be sure to check for the latest before starting your search for a broker.

Identifying what you want in a broker seems as if it should be simple. You want someone to buy and sell shares for you as cheaply as possible. But there is a bit more to it than that, and there are a few more questions that you need answered before making your decision. We're all different. We all wear different clothes, live in different types of houses… why, some of us even like flock wallpaper and swirly carpets. In other words, we are all likely to have different requirements of our broker. What follows is an attempt to nail down those requirements and get them in some kind of order.

First, Take Two Sheets of Paper

As an Internet-based company, it is obvious that our credo must be the paperless society. It forms the centrepiece of our beliefs. We'd be crazy to say anything else. So… here's what we suggest you do: take two blank sheets of paper and draw three columns on each.

On the first sheet, head the columns: 'Essential', 'Bonus' and 'Unimportant'. This is your 'Broker Selection Criteria' (or BSC) sheet. The three columns on the second should be headed 'Broker', 'Pros' and 'Cons'. This is your 'Selecting Your Broker' (or SYB) sheet. The first column on your BSC sheet is for the aspects of broker service that are essential to you. The second column is for those facilities that you would like to have, but which you can do without if necessary. The third column is for listing those criteria that you just don't need.

When you have been through all the criteria listed below (and any extras that are important to you) and you've finished scribbling on your BSC sheet of paper, you will have set out a baseline which will help you pick a broker. That's when the Selecting Your Broker sheet comes into play. Using your completed BSC sheet, go through the tables you'll find in the Getting a Broker section at the Motley Fool online and select those brokers which meet your criteria.

Add the names of these brokers to your SYB sheet. As you consider each broker, the chances are that one broker will offer slightly less or more than you wanted in certain areas. This information goes down in your 'Pros' and 'Cons' columns to help you decide later.

Then, See What Fellow Fools Are Saying About the Brokers

When you think you're finished with your SYB sheet, stop by the Brokers message board. You'll find it within the Managing Your Finances message board folder at the UK Fool site and there you'll be able to see what kinds of comments your shortlist of brokers are attracting. If they're universally getting slammed for customer service, think again about whether you want to include them. If everyone has nothing but good to say about a particular one, then jack that broker up a notch in your estimation. You may find there are no recent comments about the brokers on your list. In which case, why not post a message yourself, asking if anyone has any recent experience or comments to add?

Now, Contact the Brokers

When you have your shortlist sorted, you need to contact the brokers concerned for an information pack and some application forms. You should also look carefully over their Web sites to get a feel for the type of company you will be employing. This is an important point. You will be employing these companies to act on your behalf, trading money which is very dear to you. You want to be comfortable with your broker, but more than that you will need to trust that the broker will be able to do the job correctly. In the same way that you choose your stocks from companies with growth potential based on a sound analysis of each company, you need to apply Foolish thinking to picking a broker. The company that you will be trusting with your money has to be a competent one that stands out from the crowd on the criteria you have chosen.

So, if this company is all you expect it to be, then surely the staff will respond to your request for information in a timely fashion, won't they? If a company is worthy of your business, it will respond to your request for details and application forms in a timely manner. UK First Class mail is normally next-day delivery, so if you make a call or send an e-mail on Day One prior to the end of business, you should expect a pack sent out at the end of that day. Thus you should expect all your responses by Day Three at the latest. Day Four if you're of a particularly generous disposition.

If you get any responses arriving after that, you need to ask yourself why those brokers took so long to respond. Are they overworked? Do they have too few staff chasing too many accounts and new applications? What does this say about the company and their attitude to customer service? If they can't be bothered to be sweet to a potential new customer, how will they treat you when they already have your account? The last thing you want is complacency in your broker.

Making the Choice

Then, in your most comfortable chair with a glass, cup or mug of your favourite brew beside you and with all details at hand, you can comfortably get down to the business of selecting your broker. If you have more questions for any of the companies, e-mail them or phone them to test the speed of their responses as well as the knowledge of their staff and the ability of those staff to give clear explanations to your questions. This will help you narrow the choice further.

Having decided which company is going to get your business, fill in and sign the application forms and send them off. You are now well on your way to investing Foolishly with the confidence that comes from having done your own thorough groundwork.

We'd just like to add one thought here. By going through the above process you will have become an incredibly informed consumer, making a sound choice on the basis of your personal needs and preferences. Through the rise of the Internet and sites like the Motley Fool, companies are going to have to deal with people like you more and more. It will be interesting to see which companies rise to that challenge and which feel unbearably threatened, for not all will be equal to the task.

Finally, once more, don't forget the Brokers message board. Go there to compare notes, ask questions or relate the experiences that you've had with your broker. And please come back later and tell us how you are getting on with your new broker. Your experiences will benefit others making the same journey in the future.

So what are the criteria that you really should be looking for in a discount broker?

Those Criteria, in Full

The following criteria are not placed in any specific order, and no prioritization is intended. Priorities are up to you. The list is also not exhaustive, and there are going to be many people who have important criteria that are not on our list. Only you will know which are important for you and which are not.

Remember, you'll find more information on what all the brokers offer over at the Get a Broker section, nestling within the Fool's School section at **http://www.fool.co.uk**. If you want the whole address, it's this:

http://www.fool.co.uk/personalfinance/ discountbrokers/discountbrokers1.htm

1. What type of account do you want? First you need to decide if you want a certificated account or a nominee account.

A Certificated Account is what you need if you want to hold your own share certificates. The broker will send you your certificates when you buy and you have to send them back when you want to sell. If you hold share certificates, you are the direct legal owner of the shares. You will receive dividends, annual reports and another information sent to shareholders directly from the company. Holding your certificates guarantees you can claim any company perks that shareholders are entitled to, and can attend and vote at a company's Annual General Meeting. The disadvantage with paper certificates is that you may find that there are delays in trading, as they have to be physically sent back and forth.

Many brokers are now holding shares electronically in what are known as nominee accounts. Your broker will register the shares in the name of a nominee company it has set up specifically for the purpose. The legal ownership of the shares resides with the nominee company, but beneficial ownership belongs to you (which, in reality, means that the shares are yours just as much as if you held the actual certificates).

Dividends will be paid to the nominee company, which will then pass them on to you. All assets held by the nominee should be held separately from the assets of the broker, so if your broker went bust, your shares should be safe. The broker will also carry insurance against fraud, which should protect you further.

One of the major problems with nominee accounts is that, as you are no longer the legal owner of the shares (i.e. your name is not on the company's register of shareholders), you will not receive any direct communication from the company. That means you will not automatically receive annual and interim reports, or any shareholder perks that go along with owning the shares. Some brokers will send reports to you, but usually only if you request them, and some brokers will charge you for doing it.

In theory, if your shares are held in a nominee account, you lose the right to attend, speak or vote at company meetings. However, in practice, most companies will let you attend and speak, although voting on specific issues will need to be done through your broker.

In other circumstances, such as a bid made to buy the company, your broker should contact you and ask for your instructions. They may only send you a brief note asking for instructions on how they should vote, without providing you with enough detail to make a decision – always ask for all documentation sent out by the company.

2. How often will you trade? You have to decide if you are going to be a frequent trader over the course of a year. If you are going to trade often, then you may get better rates by paying a higher annual account fee in return for lower dealing charges. This may be for you if you are going to trade, say, more than ten times a year. But if the company charges for such a service and you don't meet the minimum number of trades, that extra fee will be wasted. Some companies offer a system where your normal annual fee is waived if you trade more than a certain number of times per year.

3. Does it have to be an online broker? Although online brokers are most convenient, you may not necessarily find an online broker who satisfies all your other criteria. If that's so,

perhaps this is a feature you're prepared to sacrifice. Perhaps, too, you want the option to use either the Internet or the phone to place your orders?

4. Will they deal immediately? Some companies will aggregate orders and deal only at set times of the day to keep costs low for small trades, but if you are going to want your orders carried out straight away, then this is not for you. On the other hand, if it meant that dealing charges for your size of trade were a fair bit cheaper, would instant dealing still be so important to you?

5. Do you want to be registered as a shareholder? Do you want company reports and interim statements delivered automatically to your door? If so, then you will need a certificated account (see above). Either that, or a nominee account with a broker who will agree to forward these on to you. If you choose a nominee account, will the broker provide this service free on request, or charge a fee?

6. Will you ever want to trade in foreign shares? If so, you need to find out if such a service is offered and how much it will cost. Some brokers will deal in US stocks from a US dollar, UK-based account. There's more on this in Chapter 14 – A Whistlestop Tour of the USA. Others might handle all world-wide stocks, and still others might specialize in the UK market plus one other, such as Ireland.

7. What do you want to do with dividends? Most companies pay dividends twice a year to their shareholders. Do you want those dividends paid directly to you, or would you like them immediately reinvested in the company? If you want them reinvested back into the company, then you need to look for a broker who offers that. Again, find out if they charge for the service.

8. Do you ever want ad-hoc statements or valuations? With an online broker, you can see how your share portfolio is doing a hundred times a day if you like, simply by logging into their Web site, using your username and password. Most offline brokers, meanwhile, provide an annual or bian-nual report on your holdings. What if you want an interim statement or valuation? Do you want the ability to get an instant valuation on some or all of your holdings? Do you mind if you are charged when you request a statement? These are all questions to ask, and the availability of an instant valuation whenever you want it is a strong factor in favour of an online broker.

9. Is customer service important? The chances are the answer is yes, but how important? If the broker does your dealing, do you care that the e-mail or phone responses you get are curt, albeit efficient? We're not saying that they will be, but if customer service is one of your essential items, pay particular attention to this as you contact each of your potential brokers to request application forms. If you seri-ously want to form a deep and loving relationship with your broker, however, we suggest you join a dating agency instead.

10. Are you willing to pay higher annual charges to get extra facilities? Most nominee accounts charge a fee based on the number of stocks that you hold. Some charge per quarter, some per half-year, others are annual. Some have minimum and maximum charges. Some charge quite a bit more than others, with the extra cost going towards paying for extra facil-ities, like low dealing charges for frequent trades, or free regis-tration as a shareholder. You need to decide if you are willing to pay higher annual charges to get those extra facilities.

11. Are low share transfer fees important to you? At some point you will have to transfer money (or shares, if you have a nominee account) into your account in order to trade. At

other times you will want to transfer money out. You may even want to transfer shares out, perhaps to an account with another broker.

Transferring money in and out will not normally cost you anything, but transferring shares in and out can. Transferring out, for obvious reasons (the broker loses custom and makes less in annual fees), is normally the direction that incurs a charge.

12. Are lower dealing charges very important to you? In many people's minds, this is the most important question, and one to which they will always answer 'Yes! A thousand times, YES!' After all, who wants to pay high charges? This question goes a little deeper, though. Really, the question is 'Do you want the lowest dealing charges when compared to all other brokers at all trade sizes?'

What you have to consider is the actual monetary sizes of the trades you will be making. Some brokers will impose minimum and maximum dealing charges. Those that don't will probably be cheaper for smaller deals, but more expensive for larger deals. If minimum and maximum charges aren't important to you, and you will be trading at high volumes, do you care that you may be paying, say, £6.50 more for a £10,000 trade? If you are only trading in very small amounts, then the absence of a minimum charge might save you £10 on a deal of £500 when compared to a broker that does impose a minimum charge. You'll need to work out your trade sizes and then check out the comparison tables at the UK Fool site to get a feel for what you need.

If you are a smaller investor, there is no reason you can't open an account with one broker now for smaller trades, and when you have built up to larger sums, switch to another broker who imposes a minimum charge but charges a lower percentage. Just check all the charges, including share transfer fees if necessary, and plan ahead.

13. Finally, what about an ISA? Independent Savings

Accounts, or ISAs, allow you to shelter any gains you make in your investments from capital gains tax. In the first year of their existence, up until April 1999, each UK resident over the age of 18 could put up to £7,000 in total into ISAs. After that, it went down to £5,000 per year. If you wish, you can invest the entire of this amount in shares. They are potentially a great thing for investors and we talk about them in detail in *The Motley Fool UK Investment Workbook*. You have to decide whether investing your money within an ISA is important to you and, if so, find out whether your chosen broker allows you to do so. Not all do.

We can't go into detail about ISAs again here, because space doesn't permit it. Also, do you want us to be brutally honest? You do? OK. You asked for it. Although the concept is good and they are a valuable concession by the government to investors, the actual details of the ISA are confusing and achingly, horribly dull. Boring. Boring. Boring. We just can't face it, OK? There are limits, you know. There's only so much flesh and blood can stand. We've done it once. Isn't that enough for you?

Sob!

It's not?!

Sob!

Just leave us alone, OK? You're not getting it!

And that's the end of it.

Congratulations! You've Opened a Brokerage Account

You've gone and done it, you Fool! You've taken the plunge. You're ready to go. Stretching ahead are possibly decades of opportunity, but as ever, do not rush. Take the time to give yourself a pat on the back and pause for breath while surveying the vista. You're well on the road.

On the issue of brokerage accounts themselves, check back occasionally to the brokers message board at the Fool. That will give you the opportunity to tell others how your broker is performing. You'll be able to air your gripes or, hopefully, proclaim your pleasure at their outstanding service. It's a world which changes very rapidly, however, and today's leaders are tomorrow's laggards. Keep an eye open, therefore, for companies offering better and cheaper service than your current broker. You may wish to change at some point in the future.

Of course, as an active, interested investor yourself, it's also up to you to keep your broker aware, via e-mail, of whether they're providing a good service to you. Tell them what the competition is offering and ask them how they intend to match it. Companies these days – especially ones trading on the Internet – love to hear from their customers. They really do. Or at least they should do.

Chapter 11

Buying and Selling Shares Online

The first thing to say is that the basic principle of buying shares is the same, whichever broker you decide to use, and whether you decide to use an online or an offline broker. The only difference is that offline you will probably speak to a broker on the telephone or send them a letter, while online you will place your orders over the Internet. This chapter presumes you are using an online broker, but if you're using an offline one, the principles are just the same.

Let's suppose you have now selected your preferred online stockbroker, you have filled out the forms and opened an account. You have even deposited some money with them so that you are now in a position to actually make a trade. (It's very similar to opening a bank account.) Further, you have done your research, you understand what you're going to invest in and are comfortable with it. You're there, you're on the brink. You're ready to buy a share. How do you actually *do* it?

If you visit the Web sites of most of the Internet brokers you'll usually find a demonstration page(s) of how it all works. It is worth running through the demonstrations at a couple of brokers to see how each one functions. After you've looked at a couple, you'll have picked up the general principles and realized they're fairly similar. Below, we are going to use a series of demo screen shots from DLJ Direct, Etrade and Charles Schwab. This does not mean we recommend using any of these as your broker – we don't make those kinds of recommendations – simply that we had to choose a selection to demonstrate the principles. It was their lucky day.

The first thing you have to do, of course, is log onto the site, using your personal ID and password. That will take you through to a page allowing you to access details of your account and to trade online. A useful page to start off from is the 'Account View' page, reproduced below. This shows details of your portfolio and how much money you've got available to trade.

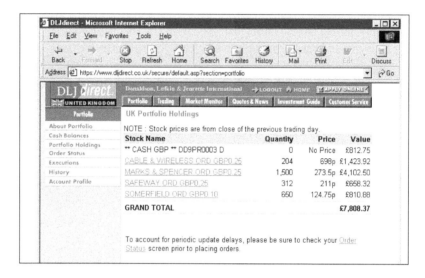

Well, we can see you're a strong fan of Marks and Spencer. A *very* strong fan. Also, we can see you have some cash available to invest. You have over £11,500 available in your account. Fantastic! This book is getting better and better.

Let's suppose you like Spreadem Chairs PLC, a company which specializes in making easy chairs for the 'generously proportioned'. They're planning to enter the US market. You know there are plenty of 'generously proportioned' people in the USA and you're saying to yourself, 'This is a company with smart management and great prospects. I want some of it!' Custom-made chairs for fat people, you think, have a terrific future. You're going to put your money where your mouth is and become a part-owner of the company.

Bravo!

You decide to buy some and hit the button which takes you to a page like this:

114

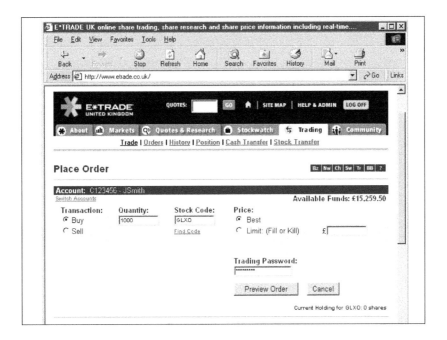

The first thing to do is fill in the share or EPIC code for the company you want (we talk about these in more detail a little further on). You don't know the code for Spreadem Chairs? Just hit the 'Code Lookup' button, enter 'Spreadem Chairs' and the answer comes back... well, would you credit it, someone *does* have a sense of humour at the stock exchange after all: it's 'BUM'![5]

Fill in 'BUM' where it says 'Enter Share Code'. Then tick the 'Buy' circle and decide whether you want to buy a certain number of shares or a certain pound sterling *amount* of shares.

You're going to commit £5,000 to BUM? Wonderful. We like the fact that you're so positive!

Finally, you have to specify what type of purchase order you want. By ticking the 'at Best' circle, you are asking the company to place what is known as a 'Market' order. This means the broker will secure for you the best possible price available in the market at the time you place your order. We don't want to break the spell, so we'll talk about limit orders

---

[5] Spreadem Chairs (BUM) is in fact a made-up company and is our homage to the *Carry On* tradition of humour and *double entendre*.

a little later and presume that you're placing a market order here.

All that is needed now is to hit the Place Order button and you're away. You'll then be faced with a confirmation screen, telling what you have bought and for how much. When you go back and recheck your portfolio, you'll find it recognizes the fact that you are now the proud owner of £5,000 worth of BUM.

If you hit the transaction history page, which any online broker should provide, it will give you the details of all the transactions you have made, a bit like this:

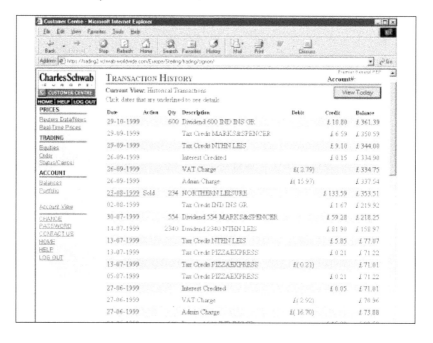

The Different Types of Order – Market, Limit, Stop

Market orders are easy. You've just placed one. The broker gets you the best available price at the time you deal. Simple as that.

Limit orders are pretty simple too. With a limit order, you specify the price at which you are willing to buy or sell the shares. Your trade will then only be completed if the broker can get an equal or better price than your limit. For instance, you can specify a purchase limit order for a share of 250p. That means you only wish to buy it if the broker can get a price for you equal to or better than 250p. If they can't get that price, you don't buy. Similarly, a sell limit order means that if the broker cannot get a price for you at or above the price you specified, they won't carry out the trade. Placing a limit order does not necessarily mean that your deal will be executed at the limit price. If the broker can get you a price better than the limit it is their duty and responsibly to ensure that they get you the very best price in the market at the time your order was processed.

It is inevitable with US online brokers rushing to enter the UK market that US share trading jargon is going to creep in over here. The term 'Fill-or-Kill limit order' seems to have arrived already with at least one broker, Etrade. With a Fill-or-Kill limit order the broker attempts to execute the trade immediately. If it cannot be completed immediately, it is automatically cancelled. Other companies will hold a limit order for you for a day, others for longer periods. Some will charge you for carrying limit orders over from the close of trading. Check with your own broker to see what they offer.

There are some other types of trades which will probably soon be introduced to online brokers in the UK from the USA. By the time you read this, they may already be offered. These revolve around the stop order. A stop order is an order which is only activated at a certain level. In other words you give an instruction to sell or buy if the share price rises above, or falls below, a pre-set level. When that level is passed, the stop order will come into effect.

The simplest type of stop order is a stop *market* order, which will guarantee execution of the order, but not the price. It may be that you have set a sell stop market order, such that if the price of your chosen share falls to 200p or less, then the shares will be sold. If a company issues a profits warning, however, or there is some other dire news, it is quite possible that the price could collapse rapidly through your stop order level to, say, 100p. Because you have set a sell stop *market* order, your trade will then be executed at 100p, well below that 200p level at which you specified the order should be activated.

Alternatively, you can set a stop *limit* order. That means the order will come into effect at a certain level, but if the broker cannot then effect a trade within the limit you have specified, it will not take place.

Don't worry too much about the more complicated stuff. For most people, and certainly for most Fools, simple market and limit orders suffice most of the time.

EPICs and Tickers

As an online investor, you are going to be talking in EPICs (UK) and tickers (US). These are short codes which represent individual shares and are used because some companies have very similar names. The EPIC or ticker refers unambiguously to one company only and prevents mistakes. Oh, and since you asked, EPIC stands for Exchange Price Information Computer (Code).

You can look up an EPIC by clicking on the Quotes/Data tab at the Motley Fool and typing the company name in the box under the yellow Lookup heading. Then click on the green GO button:

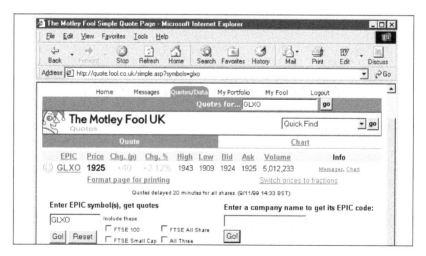

Your broker will have a similar facility.

It is important to notice that some EPIC Codes have a full stop in them (for example, 'BG.' for British Gas). This is an important part of the code and must not be forgotten.
The full stops are there because in the UK all EPIC codes must have a minimum of three letters.

In the USA, stocks trading on the NYSE (New York Stock Exchange) have one-to-three-letter symbols, stocks trading on NASDAQ (National Association of Securities Dealers, Automated Quotations) have four-letter symbols, and mutual funds have five-letter symbols ending in X.

Sometimes, a company may have more than one type of stock, which is usually indicated by an extra letter tacked onto the end (like 'A' for Class A stock).

(Yet) Another Pound of Flesh – The Bid-Offer Spread

Often, when you check share prices at various sites on the Internet, you will only see one price for the shares, known as the mid price. This is also the price that is reported in most of the newspapers. Buying or selling, however you will emphatically not trade at the mid price. You have to sell at the bid and buy at the offer prices.

In simple terms, the bid price is the price at which a market maker will buy a share from you, and the offer or ask price is the price for which they will be willing to sell a share to you. 'What is a market maker?' I hear you ask, 'and why is he offering to buy or sell me shares?'

When you buy or sell a share you have to do so via a stockbroker. It is the broker's job to contact the people who actually make a market in the shares you want to buy, the market makers. There may be a number of market makers in any one share, and it is the role (and duty) of the stockbroker to get you the best price if you are buying (the offer price) or if you are selling (the bid price). As a general rule, the more market makers there are in a stock, the smaller the difference between the bid and offer prices. The difference between the bid and offer prices is called the spread. Essentially, this is the profit margin for the market maker. See where the 'pound of flesh' thing comes in?

Let's now have a quick look at two companies to illustrate a few points about bid-offer spread. One is the biggest company by market capitalization fully listed on the London Stock Exchange, BP Amoco which is valued at about £115.7 billion, and the other is the smallest capitalized company fully listed on the London Stock Exchange, Alldays, which is worth about £31 million.

Alldays has seven market makers for its shares. On a typical day, the best bid was 68p and the best offer was 73p, making a difference of 5p or 7.4 per cent of the bid price. BP Amoco, which has 239 market markers, has a best bid price of 1195p and a best offer of 1197p – so the spread is only 2p, or 0.17 per cent of the bid price. That's what competition does.

The bid-offer spread reflects a number of things. While a large bid-offer spread suggests higher profits for the market maker, that's not quite the whole story. That large spread also reflects the risk that the market maker is taking. For example, with a smaller, more thinly traded company, the market maker is taking the risk that he may buy the shares from you but then find himself unable to sell them again. In order to do so, he may be forced to cut the offer price. This obviously eats into any potential profits and may even force the market maker to take a loss. The market maker factors this risk into the spread. Market makers are obliged to make a market in the stocks that they trade, so even if the share price is in freefall and people only wish to sell, the market makers are forced to keep on buying. Of course, they will adjust the price they are willing to pay down and down until people no longer want to sell. So for companies where the liquidity of the shares is not so high (in other words there are far fewer trades made in them), the risk is greater and the bid-offer spread tends to be correspondingly greater.

This is important, so if you're starting to glaze over, have a cup of coffee and read on.

You can see that the bid-offer spread can take quite a large chunk out of your money. In Alldays' case, if you decided to buy and then immediately sell (very un-Foolish, we might add), you would lose 7.4 per cent straight away. In addition, you would have to pay your stockbroker commission, which for a small trade of £1,000 would be a minimum of 1.25 per cent. Since this is on both buying and selling, you would have paid your stockbroker 2.5 per cent in total. You will also have to pay the government 0.5 per cent of the purchase price in tax (stamp duty). In total you will have lost 10.4 per cent. Looking at this another way, if you buy shares in Alldays at 73p, the shares will have to rise to an offer price of 81p for you just to break even.

It is interesting to look at the table below taken from the report of the working group on smaller quoted companies commissioned by the Treasury, which shows the average spreads for the different FTSE stock market indexes and also for the AIM. (AIM stands for 'Alternative Investment Market' and is a stock market parallel to the London stock market, which contains generally smaller and riskier companies.) They are listed in descending order of size – the FTSE-100 contains the largest companies and the FTSE Fledgling and AIM, the smallest:

Index	Typical Quoted Spread
FTSE 100	0.6%
FTSE 250	1.8%
FTSE SmallCap	3.8%
FTSE Fledgling	8.5%
AIM	13.2%

What this table tells us is the percentage of our investment which is on average eaten up by the bid-offer spread when trading in these shares. A 0.6 per cent spread with FTSE-100 shares – that's companies like BP Amoco, Glaxo Wellcome and BT – isn't bad at all. But spreads of 8.5 per cent or 13.2 per cent for AIM shares?

Ouch!

Double ouch!

Remember that the long-term return on investing in the stock market has been about 12 per cent per annum. We have already seen how by buying and selling Alldays in one day we have lost 10.4 per cent, a very significant amount. This is why here at the Fool we encourage people to buy and hold shares for the long term. Trading charges really hurt. It's also one reason why we encourage people to avoid so-called penny shares. These are companies of small size which, apart from having difficult to forecast futures and often poorly reported financial histories, are subject to spreads far nearer 10 per cent than 1 per cent. Our rule of thumb is to avoid companies whose share price is less than 50p or whose market capitalization (total value of shares in issue) is less than £30 million.

Are Stop Losses Foolish?

With the extra flexibility that online brokers offer, sooner or later most investors are going to wonder about using Stop Loss orders. But what are they, and are they Foolish?

The first answer is quite simple. All a stop loss order does is instructs your broker to sell some shares for you if the price falls to a certain value. The level at which you set this price is known as the 'stop loss limit'. Online brokers will often accept stop loss orders and handle them automatically, though many people operate the same strategy by watching their share prices carefully and executing their orders manually.

The theory is that if we set a stop loss limit of 20 per cent below our buying price, the very maximum that we will lose is 20 per cent. By doing this we should be able to achieve the investor's dream of cutting our losses and maximizing our profits. Sounds simple, doesn't it? And the idea does have an intuitive appeal, don't you think? There are problems with using stop losses, though, but first, let's look at two popular variations on the stop loss theme.

The simplest stop loss strategy is to set a stop loss limit at, say, 20 per cent below your buying price. If the price falls to 80 per cent of the original buying price, then you sell. Nice and simple. But what if you are several years into an investment and the share price has appreciated nicely so far? Would you want to wait for the price to fall all the way back below your original buy price before you sell? No, of course not. A refinement, then, is the idea of a trailing stop loss. You set the stop loss limit at, say, 20 per cent below the highest level that the shares have reached since you bought them. So, if you buy some shares at 100p and they subsequently increase to 150p, you reset your stop-loss limit to 80 per cent of 150p, or 120p. If the shares fall to 120p you sell them. This is harder work, of course, as you need to keep adjusting your stop loss order every time the price rises.

To get back to the important question, are stop losses Foolish? On the face of it, making sure you sell your loss-making shares at a minimum of, say, 20 per cent less than their peak seems compelling, but can you consistently achieve that? Unfortunately, no, you can't. Think about what happens when a company releases bad news. Firstly, when is the news released? Company news releases are usually made early in the morning, around 7:00 to 7:30 a.m., before the stock market opens for the day, and you can't sell your shares then. Now think what the market makers, who have their float of shares in that company ready for trading when the market opens, are going to do. Are they going to open the day on the same price that they closed the previous day and wait for you to sell off your shares at a good price? No, of course not, they are going to slash the price immediately and start the day at a much lower price than the previous day. Will they cut the price by more than 20 per cent? If it is bad news, the answer is often yes, by much more than 20 per cent. So what chance do you have of your stop loss order triggering at the price you want? Precisely zero, that's how much. There are many examples, littering the pages of stock market history, of share prices being marked down 40 per cent, 50 per cent, 60 per cent or more as soon as the market opens. So, you are not going to hit your 20 per cent every time. But what about those tipsheets and newsletters whose record shows them always hitting their stop loss targets? Hmm, maybe their trades are imaginary and aren't based on what they could have achieved in practice. Fools should be sceptical.

'So sell at the stop loss limit and buy back in at the bottom,' we often hear people cry. And that highlights the other problem, probably the bigger one. Often, a stop loss order will have you selling out a share just before it hits the bottom of a minor dip, before it starts to rise again. Look back at the share price history of any really great company over this century, and see how many times its share price has fallen back by that 20 per cent stop loss limit. Plenty, we'll wager. And each time, how far did it fall before rising again? Often, not much further than the 20 per cent, and the same goes for any limit; 10 per cent, 30 per cent, or whatever.

So if you always know when to call the bottom of a share price dip, and can sell out and buy back in at the right point every time, then stop losses might be useful. But if you know how to achieve that consistently, then you won't be reading this book in the first place, will you? No, you'll be relaxing on your yacht in the Caribbean, enjoying the fruits of your expertise. You won't be jostled by any other gin palaces either, which should tell you just how tough it is to time the market correctly.

Chapter 12
Keeping Track of Your Money and Investments

There always seems to be so much going on these days that it's terribly easy to lose track of exactly what is happening to all our money and finances. That's potentially a fatal mistake, however. If we don't know how much is coming in and how much is going out, we're in no position to decide how much we're able to save. If we don't know how our investments are performing as compared to the stock market index, we're unable to say how well we're doing. Neither of these situations is a good one, which is why we're going to look at some of the ways in which you can keep track of your £££££.

There are three things we're going to look at:
• Tracking your investments on the Internet.
• Tracking your finances using specialist software on your computer.
• Online banking.

Does this sound like a lot? Don't worry, they all tie in well and the truth is that, apart from being crucial for any investor, having a good handle on what's happening to your money will make you feel happier and good about yourself. It's worth the relatively small effort to set all these systems up and keep them going. Try it!

Tracking Your Investments on the Internet

The Internet is a great help in investing. That's pretty clear by now. It acts as a terrific resource for company research and a wonderful place to exchange ideas with other investors. But actively investing on your own behalf, by which we mean investing in individual shares, is a long-term business. Just investing some money into a company isn't enough. You

125

have to keep your eye on what's happening to those companies in whom you've invested your future and make sure they're staying on a track of which you, a part-owner, approve. You want to know if they've met their earnings targets this year, which other companies they have decided to buy, whether there's been a change in corporate strategy you may not entirely agree with, or a host of other things. If your company isn't on track, you'll want to know why and if that reason doesn't satisfy you, you may want to reconsider your position, perhaps selling it and buying something you think is better.

How often to keep track of the individual shares you own depends both on your personal inclination and the types of holdings you have. There are some people, holding solid, dependable FTSE-100 companies, who like to check how their shares are doing twelve times a day. Others, with more speculative, riskier holdings, may be altogether more sanguine. There is no hard and fast rule for how close an eye you should keep on your investments. As with so much in Fooldom, it's up to you to figure out what types of companies you want to invest in and then how closely you feel you need to monitor them.

What's the most basic way to monitor your shares? By looking at the share price. You can do this by entering in the company name or EPIC symbol at any number of quote boxes on the Internet, of which the Motley Fool of course has one. At most of these sites, including the Fool's, you'll find the prices are delayed by roughly 20 minutes. That level of delay should be bearable for all but the most hardened day trader. If you find you need real-time share prices on which to base your long-term investment decisions, go back and read Chapter 4 to make sure the bogeyman hasn't got you.

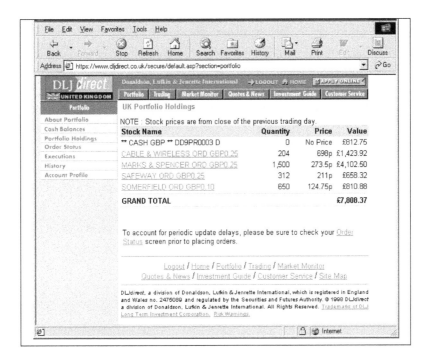

Easier than entering the share price of each of your companies every time, is to set up a portfolio. If you hold your shares within an online brokerage account, you will probably be presented with a snapshot of how your companies are doing each time you log into your broker's site. Most online brokers will also allow you to check your transaction history for the shares that you have bought and sold through their site. In addition, you will generally be able to order statements.

There are many other places on the Internet, apart from your broker, where you can set up a portfolio, including the Motley Fool. Currently at the Fool, you can only enter shares into your portfolio, but some other sites, including Interactive Investor (**http://www.iii.co.uk**) and Moneyworld (**http://www.moneyworld.co.uk**), do allow you to enter other types of investment, such as unit trusts. Portfolio tools are becoming more and more sophisticated all the time, offering customizable charts, links to company fundamental reports and company analysis and will track your performance against the index.

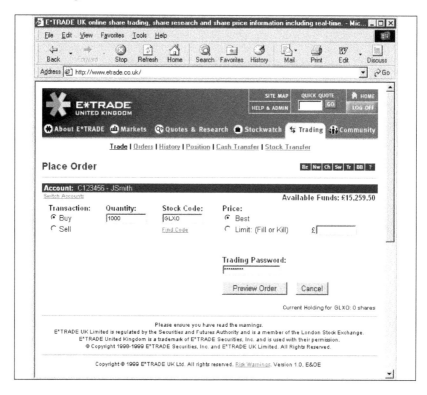

Of course, if you're just investing in an index tracker, you'll have no problem at all in keeping up with the general performance of your portfolio. All you need to do is listen to the radio, watch the TV or log into just about any financial site on the Internet to find out the current value of the FTSE-100, which is what your fund is likely to be tracking. Even if it's tracking the FTSE All-Share Index, the level of the FTSE-100 will still give you a good idea of how you're doing, as the two mimic each other fairly closely. All this said, an index tracker investor has the least need of any stock market investor to monitor the performance of their investment. The short-term ups and downs of the stock market are utterly irrelevant to the long-term outcome of your investment. You want some Foolish advice? Switch the market off. Don't listen. Forget what the Footsie is doing. Instead, just get on with your life, keep contributing what you can each month and smile wryly at the rest of us Fools, surreptitiously logging on to check the value of our portfolios far too frequently.

You've got your portfolio set up. What next? (Sorry? You checked it how many times yesterday? Well, that's OK. Just *checking* is fine.) What happens next is that you want to keep an eye open for any news on the company. On the other hand, why duplicate something many, many other people are already doing? Once again, the awesome thing about the Internet is the way in which it allows a collaborative effort to far surpass the efforts of each of us acting on our own.

It's a fair bet that if you keep a close eye on the message boards at the Motley Fool that relate to the companies in which you own shares, you'll pick up most of the important news pretty soon after it first breaks. There are thousands of other Fools out there, many of whom own the same shares as you do. It is almost certain that someone will spot a news story on 'your' company and will post a message about it on the message board, often including a link to the story itself in the posting. It's a much better way of keeping up to date than just scanning the stories on your own. Of course, it's down to you to help in this process by keeping your eyes peeled for anything interesting on the companies that you are following. When something pops up in a print newspaper, or on one of the online news services, post a note on the board telling everyone else.

Knowing how much cash you have, the value of your investments and the performance of your portfolio in comparison to the market indices really is important. You have to keep track of how well, or how badly, you are doing. If you are unable to beat the market performance over time, you need to consider investing your money in an index tracker fund. Some portfolio facilities, as we've seen, will allow you to compare the performance of your own portfolio against a stock market index of your choice.

Setting up a portfolio on the Internet is the work of only a few minutes, but doing so is a vital part of online investing. In fact, even if you don't have any investments yourself at the moment, you should set up an online portfolio simply so you can track the ups and downs of a group of shares you're interested in. Watching the triumphs and the tragedies, the joy and the sorrow, when you *don't* have any money invested is a uniquely educational experience. It may stop you over-reacting, in either panic or exuberance, when you do finally have shares of your own.

Tracking Your Finances Using Specialist Software on your Computer

We've talked about tracking your investments on the Internet, but there's a lot you can do with your computer before you even connect it to the Internet. Some people reading this may be used to life without a computer, but I wonder how we ever survived without them. It is amazing to me to think that when I went to university in 1979 the personal computer as a concept barely existed. OK, I had used a Sinclair computer – remember them? But who could actually own up to doing something useful on one?

During my time at Manchester University I remember seeing the first Apple computer in a showroom. It was hellishly expensive, but it was a miracle. When I left university in 1982 the first IBM Personal Computers were starting to be introduced to the workplace. I got my first PC in 1983 and I was so proud to be sitting at my desk at work with this monster in front of me. It may have had a green video display unit, nothing more than a couple of floppy disk drives – no hard disk drive – and memory that was almost non existent, but it enabled me to do things that I had not even been able to dream of before.

Now, nearly twenty years on, as we hit the twenty-first century, I sit typing this book on my laptop computer, which has more power and abilities than the supercomputers that I used at university. And before our younger readers start to think I am getting starting to sound like an old grandad, remember we are only talking about a few years ago.

Almost everyone now has access to a computer. Indeed many families have a PC at home, and very soon we will perhaps be able to say that *most* families have a PC at home. Not only can that computer be used to access the Internet, but it can also be used to actively help in managing your personal finances as well. Computers are good at number crunching and what is personal financial planning if it is not all about juggling numbers?

If you pop into your local computer superstore you will find shelves full of accounting and financial programs. Walk directly past these. You see, conventional accounting packages are next to useless at managing personal finances and trying to run your family budget using an accounts program will lead to nothing but despair.

What you need is a program like *Microsoft Money or Quicken* from Intuit. These allow you to control your entire

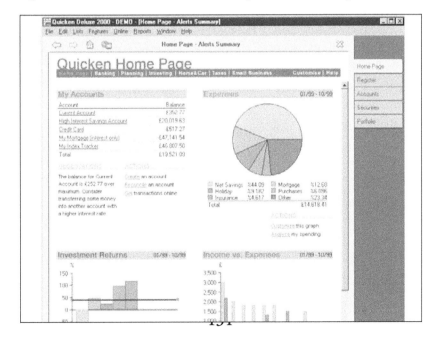

financial position. They help you to understand where your money goes. How much did you spend on food last month? How much has your car cost you since you bought it? How much money have you earned this year? How does that compare with how much you earned last year? Managing your money with *Microsoft Money* or *Quicken* will help to give you the answers to these questions and many others.

At this point in time, these may not be questions you'd particularly like to have the answers to. That's understandable, but you know in your heart of hearts you really should keep track of all these things.

Come on, you do know that really, don't you? You do …

Stop playing coy, you old rogue.

…

Using a computer with a program like this is by far the easiest and most effective way to keep your financial life in order. Good record-keeping is also essential for tax purposes. You need to know exactly how much you earned, how much interest you have received in the course of the year and also how much you paid for an investment, when you bought it, how much you sold it for and exactly when you sold it.

Both *Quicken* and *Microsoft Money* will handle all your financial chores for you, including helping you balance your bank account, savings, and credit card accounts. They'll also help you to devise (and hopefully stick to) a budget, create reports and charts for your expenses and revenues, pay your bills electronically, receive bank statements over the Internet, transfer funds and more via online banking, notify you of bills that need to be paid soon, plan your retirement, teach you how to knit an Aran sweater, impart the finer points of the Norwegian playwright, Ibsen, and a whole lot more.

How do you use these programs? Well, installation is quick and easy, and in general setting them up is not too difficult. The first thing you need to do is to create the various accounts which they'll prompt you to create and type in the balances. For example, how much you have in your Foolish savings account, how much you owe on your credit card, how much you have in your current account, and so on. Then you can type in expenses as they come. For example, the amount you spent filling the car up with petrol, or how much you spend on food at the supermarket.

You will have some regular payments, such as the mortgage or the electricity bill, and these can be planned, you can tell the programs when they are due, and you will be reminded. You can also see how the payment of future bills will affect your future bank balances, and this will tell you if you need to cut back your expenditure to keep your bank balances in the black.

You can also set up your investment portfolio to show you a summary of your current investments. You can manually update their values, or you can update them via the Web. Press a button and the program will connect to the Internet, retrieve the quotes and update the current prices of your investments. You can also produce many different types of charts and graphs that show you where you are earning your money, and where you (or your partner – that's always good for a bit of strife) are spending it!

Of course, if you are a dab hand with a spreadsheet like *Excel* or *Lotus 123* you can set up simple spreadsheets to do roughly the same thing, in which case you really don't need to use a money management program to help with your financial planning. For the rest of us, though, they are useful, essential almost, and if you're having any problems stop by the Financial Software message board at **http:// www.fool.co.uk** for help and guidance. You'll find it in the Managing Your Finances message board folder.

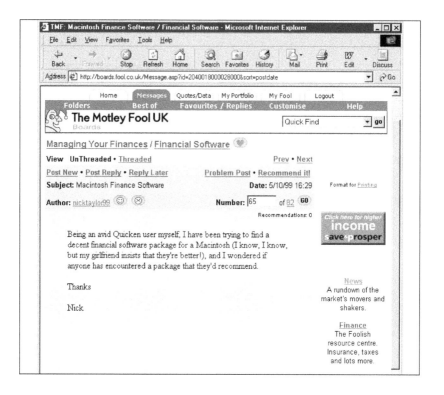

Online Banking

Let's take everything we've learned in the previous two sections and throw an online bank into the equation.

Online banking is not new. In fact it has been in existence for over fifteen years since the Royal Bank of Scotland pioneered their home and office banking service, called HOBS. Internet banking has enormous potential for the banks and for their customers. At the moment few people actually bank online, but with the rapid growth of the Internet that is changing very rapidly.

Online banking is a perfect application of the Internet, and the banks are beginning to recognize that they can offer a lot more to their customers at a lower cost to themselves. Not surprisingly, most of the existing banks were initially slow to grasp the significance of the change that is happening, but are now working very hard to capture market share in the future. But they have a problem. The high street banks have outlets on every high street in the UK, a network of offices into which they try to entice you. There, they try to sell you various financial products. It has been the way they have done business for years, but this is an expensive infrastructure and increased use of the Internet for banking represents a major threat to this tried and trusted way of doing things. How happily will the high street banks embrace this new banking medium, in the knowledge that it will probably scalp their offline business not too far down the line? Perhaps the question for them, though, is whether they can afford not to adopt it. There's no doubt about it, the Internet is brings hard choices for businesses as they decide how they are going to adapt.

So what is Internet banking all about? Well quite simply, by using the Internet you have the ability to link your computer directly with your bank. All the major high street banks now offer some kind of e-banking solution. Some of these are fully fledged Internet-based banking solutions, others are 'computer banking' in which you connect to your bank down a dedicated telephone line, much as you dial up your ISP.

The idea of online banking is that it gives you greater flexibility. Very few people know their bank manager or visit their local branch to arrange simple financial transactions these days. Most people now do this over the telephone, or use the cashpoint machine, and this is a trend that will continue in the future. The use of Internet banking means that the majority of the financial tasks that we want to perform can be carried out from our home or office using a computer at any time of the day or night. With an Internet bank account you can check your account and see all of your transactions on screen. You can check balances, print out statements and pay bills. You can transfer money between accounts and you can buy insurance and other financial products. Some banks also have their own online brokerage. Internet banking allows you to take control of your finances in a way that has never been possible before. You can even access your account from anywhere in the world at any time as long as you have use of a computer linked to the Internet.

'But what about security?' Came the anguished cry. Because of the security worries a number of banks have shied away from providing full Web-based account access and have used direct dial-up connections with a dedicated phone number. In other words, you don't connect through your Internet Service Provider, but your computer dials up the bank directly. However, it will probably only be a matter of time before all online banks use the Web as the primary way of connecting to their customer.

Browser compatibly is an issue when banking over the Internet, as sites are designed to use the highest levels of security possible. They work well under the latest versions of *Microsoft Explorer* and *Netscape*, but other browsers may not let you access your accounts.

Some banks are now starting to integrate their services with *Microsoft Money* and *Intuit Quicken*, which enables you to completely computerize your financial affairs. Imagine being able to know how much you have spent at Sainsbury's on food this year, and how much more you have spent on petrol this January compared to last. This sort of detail in your personal finances will seem entirely normal in just a few years time.

One final thing. The time it takes to get all the information set up correctly, especially if you are using a bank that links into *Money* or *Quicken*, can be quite significant and setting up the details for online payment of bills can be quite time consuming. That makes it important to choose your bank with care. You're not likely to want to shift around too often.

Chapter 13
Getting the Best Out of the Fool

We're well into the book and have mentioned the Fool UK Web site many, many times, but haven't yet gone into the kind of gritty detail we think it deserves.

Fret no longer, Foolish reader, for The Advertorial has landed!

In this chapter, we'll be running through the face we present to the world on our Web site. We're proud of the site and of the community of ordinary Fools which thrives within it, helping each other learn about money and investing and enjoying life as they do so. If that spills over into extra-flowery prose or embarrassing eulogies, please forgive us and put it down to a little youthful exuberance.

What exactly are we trying to do in the small corner of cyberspace which we have created and which many people now regularly visit and call their own? Quite simply, we aim to provide a place where people can come and learn about money. We hope to offer a selection of useful, down-to-earth, Foolish articles on many different topics and on the other, a forum in which anyone – novice or expert – can feel comfortable about discussing anything to do with investing. (People discuss lots of other unrelated things, too, in a number of areas of the site created for that purpose.)

Things move fast on the Internet and by the time you come to read these words, many things are likely to have changed on our site, which we are constantly updating.

Where should you start? Well the first thing to do is log on to the Internet once more. You can then plug in the addresses (called 'URLs', remember?) and click on whatever needs to be clicked on as we go along.

Are you sitting comfortably? Then we'll begin.

Yep, that's it. Switch it on. Takes ages to start up, doesn't it? Double click to open your browser.

Click 'Connect' in the dial-up connection dialogue box which has flashed magically onto your screen.

Dialing tone… Xhurrrrrr… Doo dee dah bee doo dah dah bee dee dah… Xhurrrrrr… Xhurrrrrr…

Zip[6].

Mother! You're online. Connected. Finally!

Here we are then. Logged on. Doesn't it feel good? Pause for a second and let some of the energy of the Internet flow into your soul.

…

Now, type **http://www.fool.co.uk** into the address line of your browser. This will take you to the Fool's home page. *Comme ça*:

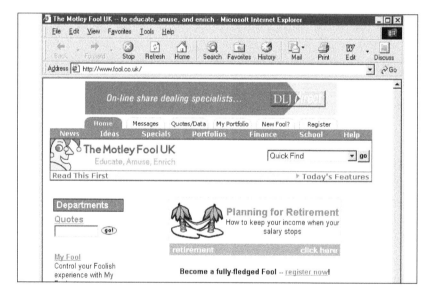

Pretty, hey? Actually, we have to admit, the Fool's site may look a little daunting at first, but it is easier than it looks to get to know the place. Broadly, there are two ways to do this. Firstly, you can click on any likely thing and see where it takes you. Then click on something else. Secondly, you can

---

[6] It doesn't really go 'zip' when your modem dials up and you finally get online, but it feels like it should.

work your way methodically and sedately through the rest of this chapter. Either way is fine and most people opt for a mixture of both, depending on how they feel at the time.

Still with us? OK, let the mad clickers do what they will. We're going to tackle it systematically and start with all the stuff we can see on the front page. My, isn't there a lot of it? Let's scan the page from top to bottom and see what we come up with.

Right at the top there is a banner advertisement. In this case it's for DLJ Direct. This is how we make the money to keep the site running and to keep expanding it. Advertisers are most pleased – and therefore most likely to keep advertising – when people viewing the site click on an ad and thereby pass through to the advertiser's own site to check out their product. If there is any advert which catches your eye as you pass through the site, feel free to click on it, but remember your browser has a back button!

Below the advert, you'll see what looks like a series of grey, unhealthy-looking teeth with large gaps in between them. Mmm, lovely. Those are meant to represent the tabs which stick out of your personal organizer. Each stickie-out tab takes you to a different section of the site. When you get there you will see a line of inner tabs which take you to its sub-sections.

In the middle of the page we have a lot of boxes. One box for each current article for that day. Our news pages change throughout the day (Breakfast Fool, Lunchtime Fool, Daily Fool). The feature articles change each day. They include articles on stock selection, our portfolios and personal finance. We also use the boxes to promote some of the content from the Fool's School. At the top of each box is a colour-coded band with the name of the area to which it belongs. The band links you to the contents or 'aggregator' page for that area.

Down the left of the front page are a variety of links to other parts of the site and the front page, in common with almost every page on the site, has a column at the bottom left headed 'See Also'. Here you will find a link to other pages which relate to the one you're on and to the appropriate area of the archives.

At the very bottom of the page are two links which remain undiscovered for many people. The 'This Week's Features' link takes you to a list of articles by day of the week.

Below the tabs is the Fool's logo, name and a little box on the right which says 'Quick Find'. It does exactly what it says, so why not now use the Quick Find box to take a tour of the site? Click on the little arrow to the right of the box as you're looking at it and then scroll down the list to find 'Fool Tour' under the Info/Help section:

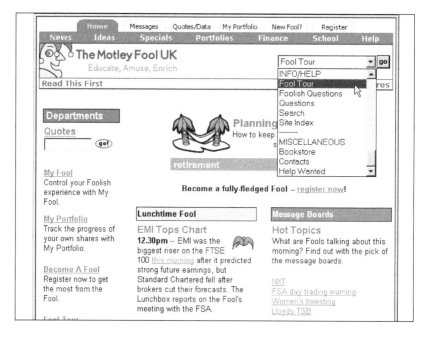

The tour will take you through most of the major sections we have, including our news, features, data and will also give you a brief taster of the message boards.

Off you go!

The Motley Fool

Welcome to the Fool

What is the Motley Fool? Founded in the USA in 1993 by brothers David and Tom Gardner, the Foolish message has been successfully transported across the Atlantic to the UK. Our name derives from Elizabethan drama, where only the court jester (the "Fool") could tell the King the truth without getting his head lopped off. In the UK for over 18 months, we've been dedicated to educating, amusing and enriching individuals in search of the truth.

"Those who understand compound interest are destined to collect it. Those who don't are doomed to pay it."

What is the truth? The stark truth is that the financial world preys on ignorance and fear. Few schools teach personal finance and investing. As a result, most folks grow up afraid to admit that they don't understand how to do things like invest in the stock market, buy a house, buy a car or handle their credit cards responsibly. True, none of these topics are great mysteries, but without a proper education, all of them can be intimidating and confusing.

But now you've set your virtual feet on Foolish soil, and your days of fear and intimidation are over. We exist to serve you, to teach you -- and to have a heck of a lot of fun along the way. We believe that:

1. You are the most capable person alive to manage your money.
2. This stuff isn't rocket science; we all just need to learn together.
3. Being smart about your money can be a lot of fun... really!
4. You can make a fortune doing it.

Take a tour | The once-over (a really quick tour) | Free registration

News | Messages | Finance | Stock Ideas | Portfolios | Fool's School

Also in the Quick Find box you will find links to:

Site index

Site map

Today's features

Search

Each of these gives the site a structure in its own way: through a keyword, through the position in the site architecture, according to the day published or through the power of our search engine.

These are all good places to go to try and find what you want on the site. If you're still lost, go to the help page where you'll find more suggestions and an e-mail link with which to contact us.

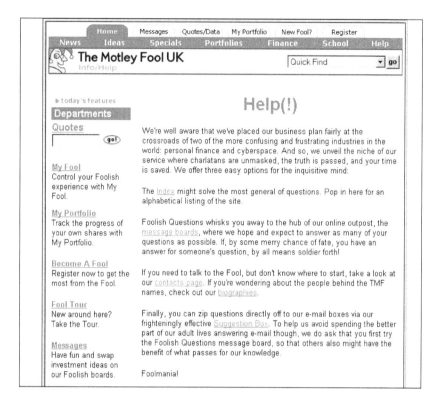

How to Really *Get the Best Out of the Fool*

Now you've been on the tour (or are sitting there panting and exhausted after a mad thirty-minute clicking session), you'll have a feel for some of the major parts of the site. That's a fine start, but what makes the Fool really different? Different, say, from a newspaper?

There's the tone and spirit, of course, along with the ethos, the sense of fun and a belief that money doesn't have to be pompous.

All that's true, but there's no reason you couldn't build those into a print publication. No, what makes the Fool – and the Internet – really different is the way in which the ordinary person can get involved with what's happening. That means two things. Firstly, you, the user, have an immediate global publishing platform for your thoughts, as we talked about earlier in the book. (No, not *those* thoughts! We mean thoughts about investing. Well, honestly…) Secondly, you can customize the Fool to suit yourself.

Both of these are simple ideas and yet so radical they represent a complete transformation in the use we make of the media. Let's look at each in turn and how to use them best. But before we do that, let's start with a look at how to register at the Fool because you'll need to do that to make maximum use of the message boards, and also to customize the Fool.

Registering at the Fool

There are a few things you have to know about registering before we start:

It's free.

It's easy.

Registering does not mean we will make your e-mail address available to anyone else.

Registering does not mean we will drink the blood of your first-born nor do any other dire things to you.

In fact, we would say it is well worth registering at the Fool because it allows you to do whichever of the following takes your fancy:

Post messages.

Recommend the messages of others.

Set up your portfolio.

Customize the Fool, including selecting favourite boards, favourite Fools and favourite places

Receive e-mail updates

So what does it entail? Simply click on the top right grey tab on the Fool's home page which says 'Register'. That will take you to the registration page:

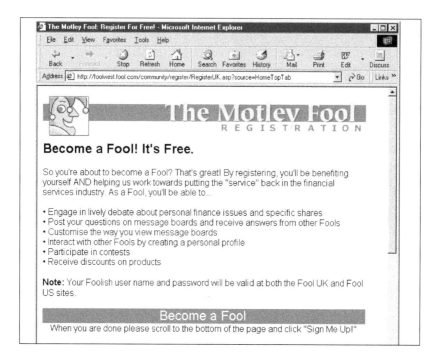

Registering is easy and the first thing you have to do is choose a user name. This can be any combination of letters and numbers that you like, but bear in mind that there are a million Fools worldwide so quite a few of the straightforward names have already been claimed. Then enter your e-mail address, confirm it and enter your post code and country. Below that section you'll find half a dozen optional questions about how you found the Fool and such like. We'd be your best friends for ever and ever if you answered those questions, but they're not compulsory and if you're cruel and heartless you'll just skip over them to hit the 'Sign me up' button at the bottom of the page.

Once you've done that, we'll send you your password by e-mail and, hey presto, you'll then be a registered Fool, poised on the brink of the greatest virtual adventure known to mankind, a cornucopia of sights and smells, of bells and whistles, nectar and honey... OK, we're exaggerating, but it's still pretty good.

The Message Boards: Your Global Publishing Platform
Traditional journalism adopts the broadcast approach, whether it is TV, radio or print. That means a few journalists broadcast their impression of what the masses need to hear, somewhat irrespective of whether that's what the masses actually *want* to hear. Of course, feedback does come through, but it takes time and is often pretty general in nature. On the Internet, however, pretty well anyone can talk to anyone and at the Fool, that process occurs through our message boards. Here, anyone – as long as they're registered with us – can post a message which could be read by anyone else in the world with access to the Internet. That makes both for a uniquely powerful form of communication amongst ordinary people and also immediate feedback for those of us working at the Fool and contributing to its content. That in turn lends a particular feel to the content which we write which distinguishes it from traditional journalism. Indeed, many of our writers have come from the ranks of message board users and we regularly feature excellent message board postings alongside the main articles as what we call 'top-level content'.

The message boards are the heart, the soul and the engine of the Motley Fool site. To get the best out of the Fool, you need to know how to get the best out of the message boards and hopefully the following sections will help show you how.

It's OK to be a Lurker
'Lurking' sounds a bit like 'stalking'. But lurking doesn't bear any relation to stalking. Stalking is what weird psychopaths do to minor celebrities. Lurking is the term used for reading postings on an Internet message board without posting any yourself.

Lurking is definitely encouraged. It helps you get a feel for what kinds of discussions are happening and who the main players are (some boards end up a bit like soap operas, with major and minor players, occasional guest appearances and the odd drama). If you lurk on a message board you may well find your question answered before you've even asked it. And not only can you lurk in the present, you can use the message board to travel back in time and lurk through an entire year or more's discussion if you wish.

But we're getting ahead of ourselves. Let's take a quick look at the message boards, pretending we're a first-time lurker. If you click on the 'Messages' tab on any page of the site, you'll find yourself taken to the message board's main page:

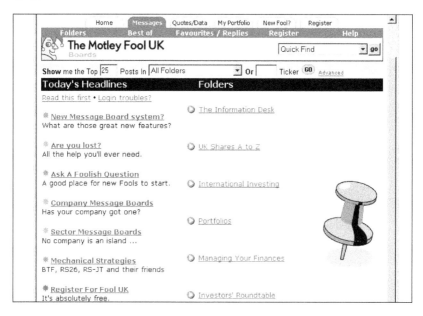

Down the middle of this page you can see the list of message board folders, which remains pretty constant, although we are steadily adding message boards within these folders. Currently at the UK Fool site we have well over 600 message boards and at the US site over 3,000. This list of folders represents rough subject groupings for the message boards:

The Information Desk
UK Shares A to Z
International Investing
Portfolios

Managing Your Finances
Investors Roundtable
Fool Café

As yet, we still have not arrived at any of the Fool's many hundreds of individual, subject-specific message boards.

But we're close. Very, very close.

Now, with the smell of our quarry in our nostrils, let's gently caress our mouse and with a smooth, yet determined stroke, one which shows we won't stand any nonsense and know our URLs from our HTMLs, move the pointer to lie above 'The Information Desk'.

Good. Well done.

Now, click.

Board Name	Ticker	Last	Total
Ask A Foolish Question		20/10/99 17:18	15483
Fool Headline Links		20/8/99 19:15	1
Improve the Fool		20/10/99 17:16	1613
My Fool		13/10/99 08:27	67
My Portfolio		18/10/99 20:45	215
Quotes & Data Feedback		20/10/99 15:02	122
TMF Book Investment Clubs		15/10/99 14:11	2
TMF Book UK Investment Guide		13/10/99 15:18	278
TMF Book UK Investment Workbook		19/10/99 21:45	13
TMF Book- Online Investing		16/10/99 11:15	202
What's New at the Motley Fool		20/10/99 17:16	62

Bingo! The message boards listed within 'The Information Desk' are pulsating gently before you, each one of them awaiting your very next click, wondering if today is their day.

Click, then, on 'Ask A Foolish Question'. This is just as it sounds: the place to ask anything you might be unsure about, whether it's to do with how to use the Fool or some aspect of investing which you're not quite sure where else to post. It's a terrific place for beginners to start. Anyway, you've clicked and at 5.30p.m. on 20 October 1999, we clicked. At that time, the AAFQ message board (as we fondly know it) looked like this:

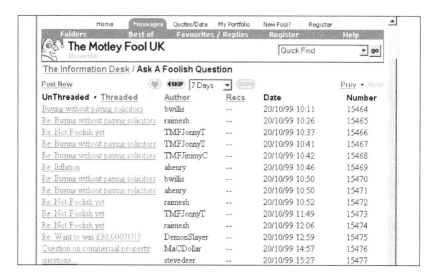

It will look different for you, of course, clicking now. Humour us, though, for the purposes of this book. You are now actually in the message board. Every item you can see listed is a message posted by someone. We clicked on message no. 15,862 by sandersj39 and it looks like this:

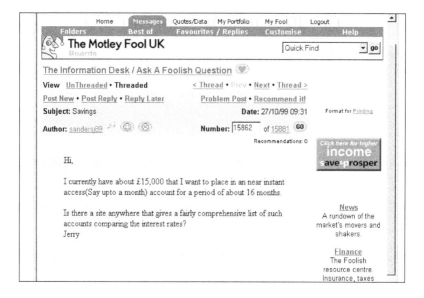

Congratulations! You are now a qualified lurker, capable of reading any of the messages posted at the Fool's message boards.

Go back to the board's main page by clicking on 'Folders' on the main tab and have a browse through all the other folders to see which message boards take your fancy. Alternatively, if you have already identified an author in whom you're interested, someone who you think posts good sense, or is amusing, you can search for their most recent posts by entering their screen name in the box at the bottom of the page and hitting 'Return' or 'Enter'. You can also use this box to bring up a company message board in which you're interested by entering either its name or EPIC symbol (see page 118).

One more thing. You may have noticed you can choose to view messages as 'Threaded' or 'Unthreaded'. What does that mean?

Well, let's suppose we have arrived at the Freeserve company message board. (We could have got there either by entering 'FRE' in the Ticker box at the bottom of the page and hitting 'Return' or 'Enter' or by clicking on 'Shares A to Z' at the board's main page, then 'Companies F' and then clicking to enter the Freeserve board directly.)

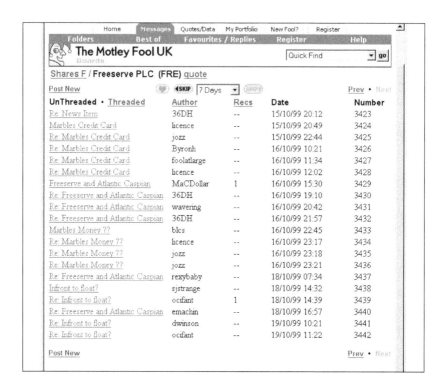

This shows the messages in order of the time they were post-ed. This is useful if you want to look for the most recent posts in a day. The alternative you have is to view the boards in 'Threaded' mode, which looks like so:

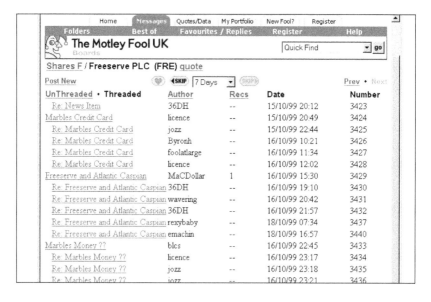

This groups messages according to the subject heading. This is useful if you've been following one particular discussion thread and want to run through all the messages. You can switch between the two at will. Go on, try it, you old devil! Give a click.

There you go. Easy, hey?

Now what else does this page tell you? Well down the middle is a column of numbers headed 'Rec'. These represent the number of readers who have recommended each message. Now the clever bit: if you click the word 'Rec' at the top of the column you will be shown the most recommended messages first. This is great when you are pressed for time.

Posting a message

Terrific! You've decided to post a message. That's excellent. We're very pleased and are convinced you'll find it a worthwhile experience. Of course, you'll have to be registered for this.

Home	Messages	Quotes/Data	My Portfolio	New Fool?	Register
Folders	**Best of**	**Favourites / Replies**		**Register**	**Help**

The Motley Fool UK
Boards

Quick Find ▼ go

Fool Cafe / **Test**

Post New   💗 ◀SKIP 7 Days ▼ SKIP▶   Prev • Next

UnThreaded · Threaded	Author	Recs	Date	Number
Message number one	TMFFatBlokeMarge	--	28/9/99 22:57	60
Stars in my eyes	LarryDuff	--	30/9/99 18:22	61
Re: Stars in my eyes	LarryDuff	--	30/9/99 18:38	62
Re: Stars in my eyes	TMFKeith	--	3/10/99 00:45	63
testing italics and bold	portfoliomanager	--	6/10/99 13:26	64
Re: testing italics and bold	portfoliomanager	--	6/10/99 13:27	65
Re: testing italics and bold	portfoliomanager	--	6/10/99 13:29	66
Re: testing italics and bold	ttgas	--	7/10/99 16:52	67
Re: testing italics and bold	ttgas	--	7/10/99 16:53	68
Re: testing italics and bold	ttgas	--	7/10/99 16:54	69
Re: testing italics and bold	ttgas	--	7/10/99 16:59	70
Re: testing italics and bold	ttgas	--	7/10/99 17:00	71
Testing	pmevans	--	8/10/99 14:57	72
Myturn	rossamy	--	8/10/99 15:45	73
Myturn2	rossamy	--	8/10/99 15:52	74
Myturn3	rossamy	--	8/10/99 16:26	75
To boldly <i>Italicize&	Station	--	10/10/99 20:58	76
Testing Quotes Problem	Monowai	--	11/10/99 14:32	77
Re: Stars in my eyes	LarryDuff	--	12/10/99 15:55	78

Now, whether you are planning to post a new message, which you do by hitting 'Post new' (surprise, surprise), or a reply by hitting 'Post reply' as you view someone else's message, let's let you into a little secret. It's this: the 'Test' message board. You'll find it in the Fool Café and it's the place to go if you're a little anxious about posting a message and want to make sure you're not going to foul it up.

You don't have to have a go at the test board first, of course, but some people do find it helpful.

OK, ready to go. Er, not quite. One more thing. From having lurked around the boards for a little while you'll have a pretty good feel for the boards and what passes for good conduct and what doesn't. We'd also like to ask you to spare a minute and read both our Posting Guidelines and our Posting Rules, which codify these in more detail:

Posting Guidelines – **http://www.fool.com/Help/Posting/Posting.htm**

Posting Rules – **http://www.fool.co.uk/Disclaimer.htm**

Now, you're ready. OK, hit 'Post New' and you get a page which looks like this:

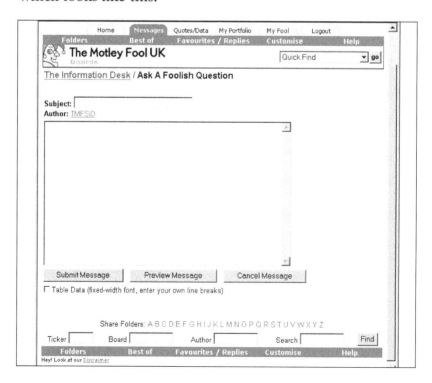

As you can see, there is a small box for you to type the subject of your message and a larger one for you to type the message itself. There is no limit on length, but messages the length of War and Peace tend to be less effective. If you want to add bold or italics, you can do so by adding the HTML tags for them just before and after the sections you want to format. For bold that means you put <b> at the beginning and </b> at the end and for italic, <i> at the beginning and </i> at the end.

Now hit the 'Preview message' button if you want to see what your message will look like when it's published. Alternatively, just hit 'Send message' to publish it.

Posting a reply is pretty well self-explanatory. The only difference is that on your reply page you will also have the text of the message you're replying to. This allows you to copy and paste areas of text from the original message and use them as a point of reference in your reply. (Remember? Highlight the area you want to copy, then hit 'Ctrl' and 'c' to copy. Move the cursor to the spot where you want to paste, then hit 'Ctrl' and 'v', *et voila!*)

One neat little trick is that if you're reading through the message boards you can click on 'Reply later' for messages you would like to respond to, but don't want to right now. Then, at the end of your session, you can click on Favourites/Replies and reply to all those posts you marked.

Assessing the Credibility of a Message

For people who aren't familiar with the Internet, this can be a big worry. How do you know what you're reading is worth reading? How do you know someone isn't having you on, leading you up the garden path on a trail of deceit, fraud and intrigue, which will finally end up with you the bankrupt victim of a sophisticated investment fraud? Horror! I'm going to be swindled out of everything!

Actually, it's not at all difficult. In the same way as you're unlikely to fall for a major scam offline, you're unlikely to fall for one online and here you have the added bonus of many thousands of other people keeping an eye open as well. Phoniness is very easily detected indeed on the Internet.

Let's get back to basics. When you're talking to someone in the pub you can usually answer the following questions pretty quickly:

'Is this one of my friends?'

'Is this person a regular?'

'Do I owe them a drink?'

'Are they drunk?'

'Have they just walked in off the street?'

These are similar to the questions you want to ask yourself online. Continuing the homely pub analogy, let's consider three situations:

1. You're in the pub, you're talking to your best friend. You trust him a lot.

2. You're in the pub, you're talking to one of the regulars who you have heard many times talking to other people, but have never chatted to yourself. You have always quite liked what that person said. You trust them, but not quite as much as your best friend.

3. You're in the pub with your best friend when in walks a stranger carrying a car radio with wires trailing. He starts shooting off a sales patter worthy of Del Boy from *Only Fools and Horses*. You discreetly suggest the landlord calls the police and checks out the car park.

Our behaviour in each of these three situations is entirely understandable and based on our assessment of it. Of course we're going to be more cautious with people we barely know. If they reliably talk good sense, however, they will go up in our estimation. If they seem about as trustworthy as Del Boy, on the other hand, we're likely to steer clear of the obvious conman.

It's no different in the online world and in some ways you have even more clues to help you identify who is worth listening to and who not. Here are some things to think about when assessing the credibility of a message board post:

Is it a user name you recognize?

If so, and if you like the person, you may even want to consider adding them to your favourite Fools list (see 'Customizing the Fool').

Does the user name start 'TMF'?

If so, that does not necessarily mean that person is an expert on this subject, but it does mean that we trusted them enough to put them on the payroll. Everyone on the TMF staff posts messages, from the newest student intern employed to shine our shoes (that's a joke), to the founders of the company. So you can trust them not to be working a scam, but don't suspend all your critical faculties. We are all just a bunch of Fools – all of us.

How many lucky charms does the poster have?

These tell you how many messages the user has posted and therefore how much of a regular that person is here at the Dog and Duck.

This is what the charms look like and they sit up next to the user's name at the top of the message:

One star for 50 posts
Two stars for 250 posts
Three stars for 500 posts
A big red star for 1,000 posts
A big yellow star for 5,000 posts

Naturally, someone with many more posts has a history of credibility built up at the Fool. You're likely to pay more attention, or at least give them more benefit of the doubt.

How many recommendations does the post have?

These are displayed on the message boards main page, in a column just to the right of the message title. They're also displayed at the top right of the message itself. Most messages attract no recommendations, so one or two recommendations is pretty good going. Five or more and 'Wow!'

Now, read the post.

This is, of course, the acid test. Is it well written? Does it contain apparently useful information, backed up by facts? Is it well argued and do its conclusions accord with common sense? Or does it display any tell-tale features of the ramper, the person who tries to manipulate a share price for their own gain? At our site we have a *trés amusant* article written by Alan Oscroft, entitled, 'The Ramper's Charter', and this details the classical features of an attempted share ramp, which often include:

• Subject of the posting is a penny stock (easier to manipulate the price, you see)
• No facts
• Innuendo and rumour
• More innuendo and rumour
• LOTS OF CAPITALS
• Many!!!!!!!!!!!!!!!!!!!
• Poorly grammered and badly speled

If you like the message, of course, you may also want to add your voice to the Hurrahs and hit the 'Recommend it' link. If you don't like it because you think it is inappropriate in some way, please hit the 'Problem Post' button and let us know why.

There's also more on ramping in Chapter 15.

Also, check their personal profile.

You do this by clicking on the name of the person who

has posted the message. This takes you through to a page which lists information about the person, including how many posts they have made, how many recommendations their posts have received and how many people 'love' them (that is have them as Favourite Fools).

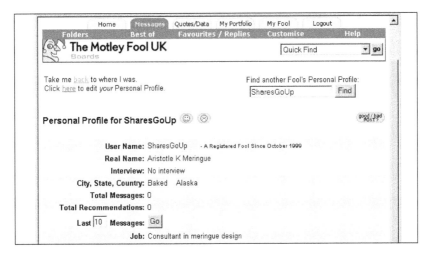

From here you can also view all their recent messages and see what the general tone of their messages has been. Not only that, but you can see how many recommendations their previous messages have attracted.

You'll find this process becomes pretty automatic after you've been reading a while and you will get to know who you want to listen to and who not. To be honest, although we're talking a lot here about how to spot untrustworthy posts, you're going to find the majority of them entirely trustworthy. A lot like this one, in fact:

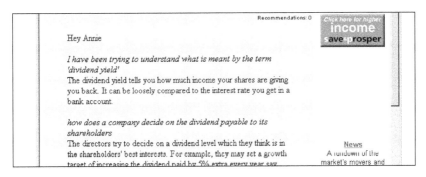

What about other message boards on other Web sites? The Fool does not have a monopoly on insight and there are other message boards on the Internet where people do post useful messages. Unfortunately, many of these boards are also inhabited by people caught up in share ramping and taking part in vitriolic exchanges known as flame wars. If you're going to have a look around at other message boards, as ever use your own judgement and decide who you want to listen to and who not.

Problems or Questions?

For message board problems, the message boards help page is a good place to start. Just click on 'Help' on the top naviga-tion bar on any message boards page. The Quick Find menu is another good place for general queries. As we've already seen, there you'll find links to the site index, site map, today's features and search functions. It may well be, however, that these are not appropriate for your question. If that's so, click on the 'Messages' tab and go through to the message boards main page.

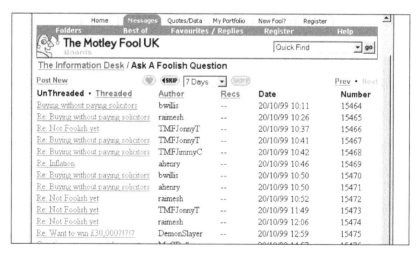

Then browse through each of the folders looking for a board with a name which you think may be relevant. The 'Ask A

Foolish Question' message board, which nestles within 'The Information Desk' folder is usually a pretty good catch-all, but you may well find other boards which have a more relevant title for your particular question.

View messages by thread and check out the FAQ[7] file if the message board has one. This is generally linked to at the bottom of the message view page and represents the most commonly asked questions and their answers in document form.

If you find someone talking good sense around your problem on the message board, click on View by Author so you can see all the other messages they have posted. Also, if you click the smiley face they will become one of your favourites and if you use View Messages by Favourite Feature you can see their posts throughout the site and not just on the current message board.

If that doesn't give you your answer you can try doing a search in the box at the bottom of the page.

If you're still stumped, post a message asking your question. Alternatively, use the e-mail address included on the help page or on the welcome message we send you.

[7] FAQ file = 'Frequently Asked Questions' file.

Viewing Recommended Posts and Most Popular Boards

Anyone can do this, registered or not. This is a great feature which allows you to view message board posts, ranked according to the number of recommendations they have received over the previous 24 hours or seven days. In other words, these are the posts your fellow users have ranked most highly. Simply click on 'Best of' on the message board's main navigation bar.

On this screen, too, is the option to view the most popular boards, 'Top Boards', graded according to number of posts made, and also to view the most recent interviews which Fools have given.

Customizing the Message Boards

Registered members are also allowed to specially customize the message boards. At the bottom of every screen, you'll see the word 'Customize' with a little red heart next to it. Click it! That will take you to a page that lists your favourite message boards.

Obviously, if this is your first time here, that page will not have any favourites on it. You'll have several clickable options:

Favourite Boards – Click here to add boards to your Favourites list. You can add a favourite board by typing in a ticker symbol or by manually choosing it from our list.

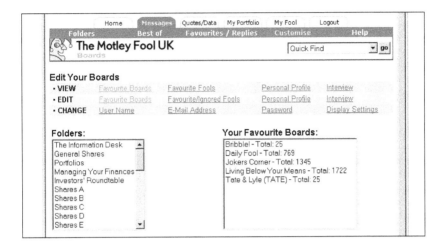

However, the easiest way to add a board to your Favourites list is when you're actually reading through the board. You'll always see a little red heart on each message board, like this:

 Click it to add it to your Favourites.

Personal Profile – We like this feature as it allows you to tell the world as much or as little about yourself as you'd like. You don't have to reveal anything if you don't want, but it's an awful lot of fun to learn a bit more about someone who you see out on the boards. You can read other people's profiles by clicking on their name inside the message boards. Chances are, before long, you'll find someone out there who has something in common with you.

Interview Yourself – Try our natty little 'Self-interview' tool. We supply the Foolish questions.

Favourite Fools – Do you have some favourite friends on the boards, perhaps someone whose posts you love to read? Add them to your Favourite Fools and you'll always be able to see their most recent posts. This way, each night, you can see what all of your friends are writing in just a click or two.

Display Settings – This group of options allows you to determine how the boards are set up for you.

161

How many Boards or Messages are shown on each page? – This refers to the number of items that show up on each page. Will you see ten messages per page or eighty-five? The default is twenty, but you can set it as high as ninety-nine per page. The fewer per page, the faster it goes.

How should the Boards be sorted? – You can sort each board alphabetically by name. This is the most popular option. You can also sort it by ticker symbol and get the tickers in alphabetical order. Sorting by last date allows you to see which boards have had the most recent activity. Finally, sorting by total will always show you the most populated boards in each area.

How should the Messages be sorted? – This is one of the most unique features we have. You can sort by Unthreaded, Threaded, or Author, as we saw in the previous section.

Change Your Password – This one is pretty self-explanatory. If, for some reason, you want to change your password, this is where you go. Submit your change and we'll fire off an e-mail to confirm it with you. Pretty easy.

Even More Customization: Favourites/Replies
When you're reading through a message board you often see messages you'd like to reply to. Doing so one by one, however, can interrupt the rhythm of what you're doing. If you'd like to store those messages for a mammoth reply session a little later, simply hit 'Reply Later'. When later comes, pop over to the page below by hitting 'Favourites/replies' on the main message board navigation bar:

Board Name	Subject of Your Post	Date of Your Post	New	
Rule Shaker	Re: SB.	22/10/99 12:02	1	View Replies
Rule Shaker	Re: SB.	21/10/99 13:34	3	View Replies
SmithKline Beecham	Re: Bad news about Avandia	21/10/99 13:32	1	View Replies
Daily Fool	Re: Shares Magazine	20/10/99 20:10	1	View Replies
Rule Shaker	Re: ARM -- Where are the trousers?	14/10/99 23:21	1	View Replies

This page not only lists the messages you want to reply to, but also shows any replies others have made to your own messages, which is a very nice feature indeed. You can also see what your favourite Fools are saying and see the level of activity on your favourite message boards.

Yet More Customization: Your Portfolio

Even before we start investing, it's a good idea to put together what we still like to call a 'paper' portfolio. This is a mock portfolio whose ups and downs you track, but in which you don't have any real money invested. If you're a registered user, you can set up such a portfolio at the Fool and it looks like this:

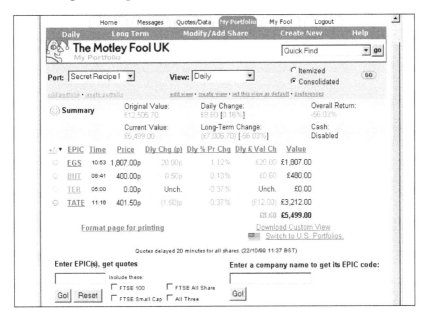

Having your own portfolio of shares set up online, whether they represent real investments or not, can be very compelling. It's fascinating to watch the prices dart around and it can be a highly educational experience too. Don't miss it. There are a variety of options for displaying your portfolio information and you can also view its long-term performance:

There's a very comprehensive help page about the portfolio feature, which you can access by clicking on 'Help' on the top menu bar. If you can't find the answer there, you can try posting a message on the Portfolio message board within The Information Desk message board folder or else e-mail **PortfoliosUK@fool.com**.

The Pinnacle of Customization: My Fool

The My Fool page can be completely customized to reflect what interests you at the Motley Fool and beyond. A lot of people actually set their browser to make their My Fool page their home page. Here's what a typical one looks like:

Your My Fool page can display your favourite message boards, favourite features, portfolio, favourite links and stock market indices. Not only that, but these are all displayed in rip off boxes. That means you can click on the small square window and then drag the box away from its current position to sit on the desktop while you are doing something else. Like so:

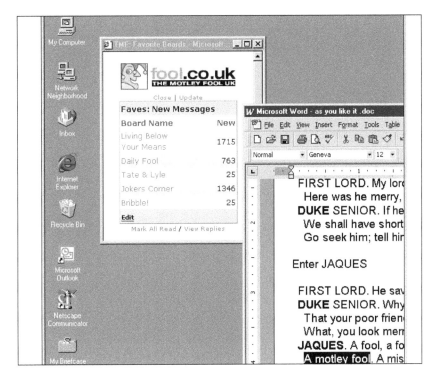

Queries about My Fool can usefully be directed to the My Fool message board in The Information Desk message board folder.

Twenty-five Things to do at the Motley Fool

Work through these on a rainy Thursday afternoon. Once you get to the end you'll be eligible for your 'Motley Fool' scouting badge. You can display this with pride alongside your 'Tricky Knots', 'Pointless Fieldcraft' and 'Membership

165

of a faintly Paramilitary Organization set up by a somewhat Dodgy Old Geezer' badges.

To make things easier, we have created a page at the Motley Fool with links to each of the things and you can find it here: **http://www.fool.co.uk/about/books/thingstodo.htm**
1. Get a price quote on your favourite share – p.85.
2. Read today's stock market news, with a Foolish twist.

3. Set up a portfolio – p.163.
4. Ask a Foolish Question – Ask a Foolish Question message board, The Information Desk message board folder.
5. Tell a joke – Joker's Corner message board, Fool Café message board folder
6. Get an investment idea – Stock ideas section.
7. Tell the world how overvalued you think Freeserve is – Freeserve message board, UK Shares A to Z message board folder.
8. Set up My Fool – p.164.
9. Save money – Living Below Your Means message board, Fool Café message board folder.
10. Discuss your favourite share – UK Shares A to Z message board folder.

11. Swap investment strategies – Investment Strategies message board, Investors Roundtable message board folder.
12. Invest like a robot – Foolish Workshop, Fool's School section.
13. Cast a vote.

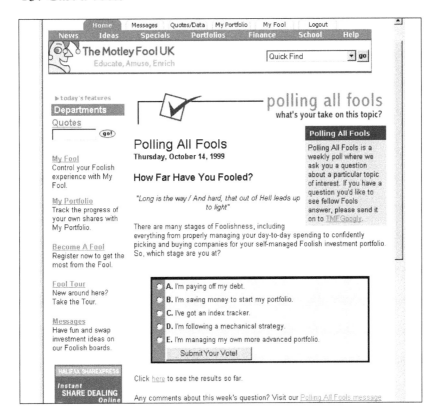

14. Tell the world what music you like by filling in your profile – p.161.
15. Recommend a message – p.155.
16. Travel the world – International Investing message board folder
17. See what American Fools are talking about – **http:// www.fool.com**
18. Make someone your favourite Fool – p.161.
19. Check out the Sector Dissector.

20. Go wa-a-a-ay off-topic – Land of Off-Topic Posts message board, Fool Café message board folder.

21. Become a value investor – Value investing sectionsand message board, stock ideas area.

22. Read the most recommended messages – p.155.

23. Talk to other women – Women's Finances and Investing message board, Managing Your Finances message board folder.

24. Swot up about tax… and like it? – Tax section, personal finance area.

25. Decide on a mortgage – Mortgages message board, Managing Your Finances message board folder.

Chapter 14

A Whistlestop Tour of the USA

Ever heard of Microsoft, Nike, Gillette, Wrigley, Pepsi, Coca-Cola, Johnson and Johnson, Disney, McDonalds, The Gap, Yahoo!? What about IBM, Kellogg, Intel, Motorola, Dell, Pfizer? All world leaders, and all Indian.

No, just kidding. They are American. You knew that.

The Motley Fool is itself an American innovation, and we venture to hope we may also be creating one of the world's future leading brands. That's a bold aspiration and time will tell, but in the meantime the Motley Fool US is a direct route into investing in the USA for anyone familiar with the UK version.

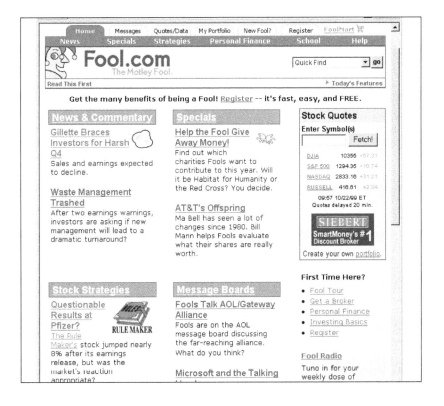

The fact is that buying shares in US companies is simple, cheap and can mean investing in some of the world's greatest brands and businesses, powering the world's largest economy. As the forgoing list indicates, we all know and understand the products of a lot of US companies. It makes sense, therefore, for us to consider investing in them.

Already, a number of UK online brokers offer US dollar trading accounts in which you can buy US shares. It is also very simple indeed to set up a brokerage account with a US-based online broker, of which more shortly.

Let's have a look, then, at the US Motley Fool and see what it has to offer. The basic structure of the site is fairly similar, but obviously the contents are entirely different.

In the news section, you'll find the latest US market news, looking at the activities of stocks on the NASDAQ and the New York Stock Exchange (NYSE). These are the two major stock exchanges in the USA. The former has most of the major Internet and technology companies listed. Microsoft and Yahoo! are listed here. The latter tends to contain more established, older companies and General Motors and Anheuser Busch, the brewery company, are listed on the NYSE.

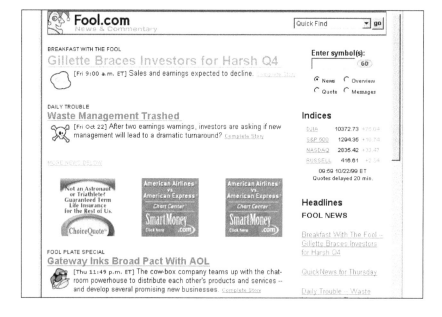

On the right of the front page you can see listed the major stock exchange indices in the USA. These are the Dow Jones Industrial Average (also known as the Dow 30) and the S&P 500. The Dow 30 represents the oldest index on the US markets and numbers thirty of the largest US companies amongst its constituents. Controversially, it is almost totally unrepresented in terms of technology stocks. The S&P 500, meanwhile, is a much broader ranging index. The NASDAQ also has its own index.

Beyond the news at the US Fool, what are most likely to be of interest to UK Fools are the stock strategies.

The US Fool runs a number of real money stock portfolios, of which the two leading ones are the Rule Maker and Rule Breaker portfolios. These each have their own stockpicking philosophy and a daily report is published on the site for each of them. The Rule Breaker looks particularly for upstart companies, those breaking the established rules in an industry sector, or even which are creating an entirely new industry sector. The Rule Maker, meanwhile, looks for those companies which dominate their industry entirely, the companies which are in such a dominant position that others have to follow them. At the time of writing, the Ruler Breaker portfolio was holding, amongst others, Amazon, AOL and Amgen and the Rule Maker, Microsoft, Pfizer and Coca Cola. You'll find screen shots of these two areas on p. 66.

Other stock strategies you'll find here include the Foolish Four, which is a mechanical, market-beating strategy, upon which the British Beating the Footsie is based, and the DRiP portfolio. The DRiP portfolio concentrates on investing small amounts into those companies which allow direct, regular, commission-free investment into their stock. It is designed for those starting out with very little money.

To help you with your stock research, the Fool's US site has well over 3,000 individual message boards, mostly devoted to individual companies. It also has more data about US companies than you could ever want, including stock charts, news, financial information, earnings estimates and more. To get company reports, though, you have to go somewhere else.

Every US company has to file quarterly and yearly reports. That's in contrast to the situation in the UK, where companies only have to tell investors how they're doing every six months. What's more, all those reports are published on the Internet for everyone to see. To access them, stop by the Electronic Data Gathering, Analysis and Retrieval system (or EDGAR), accessible from the Web site of the US Securities and Exchange Commission (the SEC), at **http://www. sec.gov**. When you get there, click on the link on the left of the page which says 'Edgar Database' and a few clicks further on you'll come to this page:

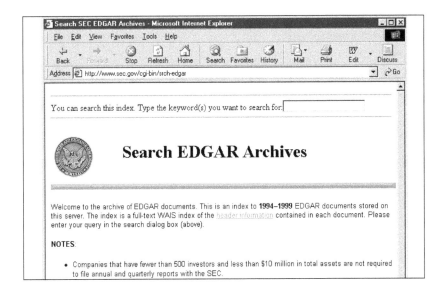

All you then have to do is enter the name of the company you want to search for in the little box at the top of the page, hit 'Enter' or 'Return' and away you go. You'll be presented with all their recent reports, which you can read online or print off and read at your leisure. Would that we had a comparable service in Britain.

Let's suppose you decide to invest in a US company. You then have three choices. Firstly, a traditional broker in the UK will probably be able to buy them for you, but it is likely to cost a lot of money. Secondly, you could open an account with one of the new UK online brokers which offers US dollar accounts and online US trading. Finally, you could open an account directly with a US-based discount broker.

If you decide on the second of these options, the best place to stop by will be the Brokers message board at the Fool UK site, which nestles within the Managing Your Finances message board folder. You'll probably see people discussing this very issue there. If not, post a question asking which brokers are currently offering US trades from a UK-based dollar account. Opening such a UK account is probably the simplest option.

The Motley Fool UK
Boards

| Quick Find | ▼ | go |

Managing Your Finances / **Brokers**

Post New   ❤ ◀SKIP 7 Days ▼ SKIP▶   Prev • Next

UnThreaded · Threaded	Author	Recs	Date	Number
Re: Internet trading	julesfools	--	19/10/99 16:56	888
Re: Best online broker ?	johnRgalloway	--	19/10/99 17:33	889
Re: Internet trading	marimo	--	19/10/99 18:05	890
Re: Internet trading	CyberSniff	--	20/10/99 11:43	891
Settlement pact	RussCox	--	20/10/99 12:02	892
Share Centre	chaurtie	--	20/10/99 13:08	893
Re: Share Centre	licence	--	20/10/99 13:15	894
Re: Share Centre	welchd	--	20/10/99 13:51	895
Re: DLJdirect offering US trades	JKew	1	20/10/99 16:40	896
Re: On-line European Brokers	sidar	--	21/10/99 13:18	897
Re: Share Centre	AliMcLeod	--	21/10/99 13:18	898
Re: Share Centre	licence	--	21/10/99 13:22	899
Re: Share Centre	jmchaffie	--	21/10/99 13:25	900
Re: Share Centre	stevensfo	--	21/10/99 13:25	901
Re: Share Centre	jmchaffie	--	21/10/99 13:27	902
Re: Schwab slipping	gkulcsar	--	21/10/99 16:13	903
New investment club seeks broker	dmdmdm	--	22/10/99 08:12	904
Re: New investment club seeks broker	licence	--	22/10/99 09:21	905
Re: New investment club seeks broker	dmdmdm	--	22/10/99 10:21	906
DLJdirect commission free until mid-Jan	spwhiting	--	22/10/99 11:53	907

Post New   Prev • Next

Opening a US-based discount brokerage account – option three – is also pretty easy, however. The place for you to go first is the US Fool's Discount Brokerage Center, where you'll find many of the US online brokers will accept overseas customers.

Although you can take care of most of the details online, you will need to sign *an actual piece of paper* at some stage of your application. That's a good thing from a security point of view. Some brokers publish their application forms online, and you can print them off. Others prefer to verify that you live where you say you do and will send you an application pack by mail. Either way, just fill them in, sign them and send them back by regular post.

You will need to pay some money into your account before you can start trading, and there is usually a minimum amount required, often around $2,000. If you have a US bank account, you can just send a cheque. If not (and most of us don't), any UK bank will be able to transfer your money electronically for a fee.

There is one more formality that must be taken care of. As a 'non-resident alien' (how nice), your taxation status must be declared to the US authorities. Residents of countries like the UK, which have a tax agreement with the US, must fill in something known as a W-8 form, and your broker should send one to you with your application pack. Just send it back with your application. If your broker did not send you a W-8, you can download one from the US Internal Revenue Service (IRS) Web site at: **http:// www.irs.gov/forms_pubs/forms.html**

If you happen to be a resident of a country that has no tax agreement with the US, then you will need to complete a different form instead, known as a 1001 form, and then no tax will be withheld. This should also be available from your chosen broker, or from the IRS Web site at the above address.

And we're not quite finished with US taxation. Do you have a genuine enthusiasm for the specific rules governing the way foreigners are taxed in the USA and wish to dedicate your life to their study? If so, you can check out IRS Publication 515 (Withholding of tax on non-resident aliens) and IRS Publication 901 (Tax treaties), also available on the IRS Web site.

Within a few days of sending all the forms and transferring your money, you should receive confirmation by e-mail that your account is open and you are then ready to trade directly in US stocks from the comfort of your own home.

How to Buy Shares All Over the World – Cheaply

Buy what you know is always good advice. In the past, that's been used as an argument against buying shares in foreign companies. Clearly, we all know a lot about the products of many US companies and there is a phenomenal amount of information available about them on the Internet.

But what about companies elsewhere? The truth is we're living in a world which is shrinking by the minute. We know more and more about many foreign companies and foreign economies, often because they're all playing in the same global marketplace. Pretty soon, it feels like there's only going to be one economy – the global one.

So, suppose you look around and decide you'd like to buy shares in Nokia Corporation from Finland, or NEC from Japan, or Deutsche Telekom from Germany, how might you go about it? You could try to find a broker in each country, of course, but that would complicate matters and might be prohibitively expensive. Using a UK broker to buy the shares listed on a foreign exchange may also cost you a lot.

There is a way, though, in which you can buy shares in all of these companies easily and cheaply. It involves using an online brokerage account which allows you to trade in US shares, whether that account is UK- or US-based. You see, many companies, including a number of large British ones, are also listed in the United States, in the form of American Depositary Receipts (ADRs). In total there are over 1,600 companies listed in the US under the ADR scheme, from more than sixty countries. An ADR represents ownership of shares of a non-US company. They enable investors to buy shares from companies around the world, without having to worry about the complex details of cross-border transactions. The ADR holder usually receives the same benefits as those enjoyed by the ordinary shareholder in the company.

One significant appeal of ADRs is that they are American, and are therefore covered by US securities regulations, which are probably the most stringent in the world. Buying and selling them is similar to the procedure for any other US share. Prices for ADRs are quoted in US dollars, and dividends are also paid in dollars.

The first ADR was created by US bank JP Morgan, in 1927, to allow Americans to invest in the UK retailer,

Selfridges. ADRs are usually sponsored by a US bank, and the sponsoring bank acts as the depositary for the original shares. ADRs are, therefore, backed by the requisite number of the original shares held by the bank.

Many UK companies have taken advantage of ADRs to get their shares listed on the US markets, and currently there are over one hundred British companies with ADRs trading in the US. These include SmithKline Beecham, Hilton Group, GlaxoWellcome and Barclays Bank. Companies benefit by broadening their potential shareholder base, increasing the liquidity in the shares and increasing their profile in the US market.

While ADRs were originally devised for US investors, anyone who can buy US shares can buy ADRs, and you can check prices and get up-to-date news, just as with any regular US company. On top of all that, you get the benefit of cheap US brokers' charges, and it can even be more cost effective to buy ADRs for British companies, than to buy the underlying shares themselves in the UK.

One final note on ADRs concerns their price. If you had checked the price, say, of Vodafone Airtouch ADRs in January 1999, you might have found that they were quoted at the dollar equivalent of £107 instead of the £10.70 quoted in the UK. The reason for that is simple. One ADR of Vodafone Airtouch represents 10 UK shares, and this differential is aimed at quoting prices at similar levels to regular US shares.

More information on ADRs can be found on the Web sites of the Bank of New York, Citibank, and JP Morgan, at the following addresses:

http://www.bankofny.com/adr/
http://www.citibank.com/corpbank/adr/
http://www.adr.com/

Chapter 15
Five Pitfalls in Online Investing

As with any revolutionary medium or idea, there is a flip side to offset the tremendous advantages it brings. In this case, the flip side is represented by a number of pitfalls deftly placed for you to stumble across in the world of online investing. With the same amount of common sense as you use in your daily life, however, you shouldn't come a cropper.

We'll start with the danger people worry about most of all and which is not only exceedingly rare, but actually one of the easiest to spot and avoid.

1. Financial Scams

The Internet is just like anywhere else. There are good people and there are bad people. Just because you are using the Internet don't let your natural 'anti-scam' avoidance techniques become switched off. You would not give £1,000 to someone who nobbled you in the pub and said he had a guaranteed, 100 per cent certain way of doubling your money in a week, so don't do it on the Internet.

The Internet is an excellent tool for investors, which allows you to easily and cheaply research investment opportunities. But the Internet is also potentially a tool for people intent on defrauding you of your money. Just as in 'real life' you should always think carefully before you invest your money in any opportunity you learn about entirely through the Internet.

Share Ramping – Occasionally, people may attempt to 'ramp' shares on message boards or in chat rooms, driving up the price of the share with their baseless recommendations and then selling their own holdings at high prices and high profits. In reality, these people are aiming to gain by selling their shares after the stock price has hit an artificial high. Once the people sell their shares and stop ramping the stock, the price typically falls and gullible investors lose their money. Con artists will use this method with small, thinly-traded companies because it's easier to manipulate a stock when there's little or no information available about the company. This kind of thing is pretty easy to spot and it doesn't take long to learn how to separate the good from the bad.

People who try to ramp up a company's share price often do so by pretending to reveal 'inside' information about upcoming announcements, new products, or lucrative contracts. They also often USE LOTS OF CAPITALS AND EXCLEMATION MARKS!!!!!!! IN THEIR POSTINGS AS THEY TELL YOU THAT SOME PENNY SHARE YOUVE NEVER HERD OF IS ABOUT TO GO THRU THE ROOF GET IN NOW ITS HOT!!!!!!!

As you can see, they don't go much on punctuation either, or spelling. It's extraordinary how share rampers will put up a message which looks almost exactly like the following and expect it to be believed:

BEAVER SOUPS GOING UP!!! TAKOVER IN THE OFFING TO BE ANOUNCED THIS WEEK

IM PILING IN

FILL YER BOOTS!!!!!

Of course, if you were a corrupt individual in possession of insider information likely to move the share price and were intent on acting on that information to make a killing, you'd be unlikely to post it to a public forum, wouldn't you? That simple fact seems to escape share rampers.

We've already mentioned the guidance notes and posting rules we have for users of our site (p.152) and if you pop along to the following address on the site, you'll find an article by Alan Oscroft, one of the Fool's writers, on life viewed from a share ramper's perspective. It makes great reading:

http://www.fool.co.uk/specials/991908ramper.htm

To be honest, ramping barely exists as a problem on the Fool UK's message boards, while being more prevalent on some other Internet message boards. This is for a number of reasons. Firstly, our 600 plus message boards can best be described as 'genteel' in character. That character comes from the people who populate the boards, the regular Fool users. These are people who have a sense of humour, are interested in learning about investing, discussing the subject, and are also very happy to help others out. They represent a community which reacts firmly to those who intrude and behave in an antisocial fashion. Our users are the overriding reason the Fool's message boards are a pleasant place to spend time.

Secondly, we have people employed to keep a general eye on what is happening at the message boards. Appropriately, these people are known as Message Board Strollers and have a 'TMF' label in front of their screen name. (Remember, though, anyone who works for the Motley Fool has such a label, not just message board strollers.) The strollers' job is to act as a helpful guide and if things do go wrong to step in and put them right. The fact is, however, that it is the ranks of our users who really provide our eyes and ears. Through the 'Problem Post' system, which we talked about in Chapter 13 – Getting the Best Out of the Fool, they alert Fool staff to potential rampers or anyone else behaving in an unpleasant manner. They also post replies to dodgy messages themselves, highlighting their nature for other users.

Although we have the power to do so, we delete posts at the Motley Fool relatively rarely, even those occasional ones which are a blatant attempt to ramp shares. This is because we think the post itself and the often eloquent replies from other Fool users and Fool staff stand as an educational lesson in themselves.

Thirdly, we don't open message boards for penny shares, companies whose shares are so thinly traded the price may be more prone to manipulation. That's actually not the main reason, however. The main reason for not opening such boards is that we think these companies generally represent poor and highly uncertain investments. At the same time, our general shares message board, where these shares can still be discussed, is not overly trafficked, meaning these messages stand out and do not get lost in the hubbub. This makes it easier for our users and strollers to spot them and respond.

Once more, though, share ramping at the Fool really isn't common and is not something you need to be overly concerned with. Most discussions are sensible, illuminating and revolve around investment strategies, the prospects of a particular company, mortgages or one of many other subjects.

E-mail Cons – Remember spam? That junk e-mail which is so easy to send? Con artists are tempted to use it to find investors for bogus investment schemes or to spread false information about a company. Spam allows the unscrupulous to target many more potential investors than cold calling or mass mailing. Using a bulk e-mail program, Spammers can send personalized messages to thousands and even millions of Internet users at a time. Always investigate information you receive about investment opportunities, get financial statements from the company, verify the claims about new product developments or lucrative contracts. Fraud online is no different to frauds that happen offline. Always be careful with your own money.

There are many specific scams out there and new ones appear too often to list them all here. A list of the major categories of Internet scam most likely to arrive by bulk e-mail, as compiled by the United States Federal Trade Commission (FTC), can be found at:

http://www.ftc.gov/bcp/conline/pubs/alerts/doznalrt.htm

You will probably recognize all the scams from the offline world too, as they include bogus business opportunities promising unrealistic returns, bogus investment schemes, chain letters, pyramid schemes, promises of free goods covering up pyramid schemes and more. A scam is a scam whether it happens online or offline. The US seems to be more prone to Internet fraud than the UK, but what starts there does often find its way over here.

That's enough about financial scams on the Internet. For anyone with the least level of discernment – and remember you bought this book, after all – they are not a major issue. They are simply an occasional annoyance and an enduring source of wry disbelief that anyone ever falls for them.

2. The Return of the Bogeyman: Daytrading

Daytrading, you'll remember, is the attempt to trade into and out of stocks on a minute-by-minute basis, trying to make money on rapid price moves. We have no sympathy with the idea and introduced the Daytrading Bogeyman back in Chapter 4. In a little more detail, here's why daytrading is a bad idea:

• It's extremely difficult to make money over time by day trading. Just as in gambling, the odds are stacked against you, and the longer you play, the more likely it is that you'll lose. You're attempting to guess which way a stock is going to move in the next few hours, minutes and even seconds. We just don't think this is possible – at least not any more possible than guessing which number is going to come up next on the roulette wheel. Any gambler can hit a hot streak; the streak has very little to do with strategy and everything to do with the law of averages.

• Just as in gambling, there is the danger that you can become addicted. This isn't Monopoly money you'll be playing with or worthless plastic chips – it's your hard-earned cash, the money you need for everything from your mortgage, your rent, your baby's clothes and the money you will need in your retirement. And like most things that are addictive, it just isn't good for your long-term financial outlook.

• Sitting in front of a computer screen all day, developing eye strain, acid indigestion and strategies for fending off panic does not seem to us to be the way to live.

• The costs can kill you. Even if you're using a discount broker, commissions can easily add up to thousands or tens of thousands of pounds when you make so many trades. Then, too, there are added costs: quote services (so you can find out instantly the price of a given stock), bid-offer spread, stamp duty and higher taxes on short-term profits.
• If you guess wrong, you've lost the power of compound returns over time, which is the best way to get – and let's talk a bit dirty here – RICH.

3. Believing '.com' Means Everything
After a little while online, you'll start to get very excited by the sheer power of the medium. The opportunities it offers for commerce, among other things, will strike you as so limitless that at some point you will have to log off, switch off your computer and just sit there in silence, basking in wonderment. Remember the Total Perspective Vortex from the *Hitchhiker's Guide to the Galaxy*? This was the machine which gave you a sudden flash of insight into just how small and insignificant you were in relation to the size of the universe. A split second of that kind of insight was enough to drive most people mad (except Zaphod Beeblebrox, but you'll have to read the books for that). Well, the Internet can have a similar, if marginally less drastic, effect.

The result of this is that sometimes people find themselves driven to invest in Internet companies, companies with '.com' after their names, simply because they are Internet companies and they love the Internet and what it can do so much.

Beware. There are bad Internet companies, as there are bad companies everywhere. In fact, why not adopt the attitude that there are no 'Internet' companies? Instead, reckon that there are only companies which use the Internet more or less effectively in communicating their message and furthering their business. Those companies conducting all or part of their business on the Internet which are good, however, and

183

which use the medium creatively and effectively may well be world beaters in the coming years.

Don't throw away your powers of discernment and judgement simply because you're dealing with the Internet.

4. Getting Too Obsessed with it All

Online investing is absorbing and fun, it really is, but there are other things in your life. Don't spend it all in front of the screen. You must allot time to finding your One True Love, relaxing with family, fulfilling yourself in a stimulating career, contributing to society, and, of course, perfecting your shove ha'penny game.

Remember that although your computer has an off button, in an emergency a stone aimed deftly at the screen will also serve.

Steady, *a-i-i-im*...THROW!

5. Not Backing Up your Data

When everything was on paper, you didn't really need to make copies. All your important papers sat snugly in your filing cabinet, safe from everything bar earthquake, war, floods or fire. Even in a fire, a metal filing cabinet would have provided some protection. You'd have been able to extract at least some singed remains.

Well, this is one place where the electronic world can be inferior. Yes, the Motley Fool admits that here for the first time. The electronic world can be inferior when it comes to keeping all your data safe and sound.

When you start investing online, perhaps banking online and keeping your accounts on your computer, you're going to end up with a lot of data stored electronically. The data stored by your broker and your bank on their computers and which you access via the Internet will be quite safe with them. They will keep multiple backup copies of all their account information. However, you are likely to have put quite a lot of that information into a program of some sort on your own machine, which you keep for your own records, such as Intuit's *Quicken, Microsoft Money* or perhaps even a spreadsheet program such as Excel.

If you don't back up that data, meaning save it onto a floppy disk, tape drive or other system such as a Zip disk, you are likely to lose it all at some point. And that's a pain. Believe us.

Chapter 16

Where Next, Share Captain?

Remember eight-track? It was all the rage back in the early 1970s, with Charles Aznavour crooning his sexy ballads out of those clonky cassettes. By contrast, the four-track cassettes seemed flimsy, a bit rubbishy. Yet today, where can you find an eight-track player and cassettes, apart from under soggy umbrellas at the nation's car boot sales? Four-track, of course, became the standard and represents the cassettes we are now so familiar with and abuse unceasingly by trampling underfoot in our cars. At the time, it was very hard to predict which would eventually win out. Many thought it would be eight-track.

Now, at this point you'd be forgiven for thinking we were going to advance some loony analogy, such as, 'You know, the Internet is the equivalent of the eight-track system and Teletext is the equivalent of the four-track system. The block colours and groovy interface of Teletext make the Internet look sick.' No way! We're not that dim, thank you very much. Teletext is useful in its own way, but there are some things it is possible to foresee and the Internet playing a huge role in all our lives in years to come and causing sweeping changes in attitudes, business and society is one of those things.

The eight-track/four-track story, however, does teach us one very important lesson: futurology is a very, very inexact science. The unfolding of events is dictated far more by luck and serendipity than by intention. No one twenty years ago could have foreseen the impact the Internet would have eventually, even though many of the elements we use today did exist back then. Because of that and because we're aware that twenty years from now these words will be quoted back to us, to great merriment we're sure, we're not going to make any specific predictions here. We'll just say this:

The Internet is already pretty important, but is only a pale shadow of what it will be ultimately. It is going to be very, very big, really huge, utterly humongous. Bigger than the Beatles, Posh Spice and the Teletubbies *put together*. Its progress will always be punctuated by surprises and it will find applications in areas which seem totally improbable today.

Will we no longer have a need for actual cash in our pockets in ten years' time because we only use 'e-cash'? Will our cars be hooked up to the network, flashing us the menus and latest special offers from the motorway services as we drive past (as if that would be a bonus!)? Will we finally put nose hair embarrassment behind us as we share our experiences with other sufferers in a virtual community rivalled only in size and relevance by the Motley Fool?

Who knows? And in some ways, it doesn't matter exactly what happens. What matters to the individual, and especially to the individual investor, is that they make sure they are well placed to benefit from what is happening now and also to help shape what comes in the future. The Internet, far from being the province of inanimate machines distant from the human experience, is a living, growing being. As a citizen of the Internet, it's up to you to get out there, use it, modify it, improve it and mould it for the common good.

Above all, using the Internet is fun. Enjoy it, Foolish reader, not only for the freedom it represents, but for the human contact it brings. Finance is already one of the areas which is most clearly in the process of transformation, but the train is still only pulling out of the station. Hopping on now will ensure you a ticket in the first class carriage, a slap-up meal in the dining saloon and even a spell on the driver's footplate for the ride of the century.

Don't miss it.

Acknowledgements

To Fools everywhere, thank you for your help and inspiration.

This book has not been written in isolation. It is in effect a partnership between myself and many tens of thousands of Fools who visit, read and contribute to the Motley Fool in the UK. Without you this book would not have been possible, and without your feedback this book would certainly not have been Foolish!

Special thanks to Alan Oscroft for helping to edit this book, and for assisting in getting it all into a sensible and understandable order. Thank you to George Row, Community Producer at the Motley Fool, for contributing greatly to chapters two and three and for making sure the user's voice was heard throughout. Also to Alistair G. Lowe-Norris, who wrote the first version of the 'Get a Broker' section on our Web site, from which I have borrowed heavily in the chapter on Selecting an Online Broker. He produced the wonderful comparative tables on brokers' costs which you will find online. Adrian Gordon produced the screenshots in a marathon couple of days: thank you.

I would like to thank all of the Foolish writers who have covered for me on the Web site over many weeks, giving me the time to get down to writing the book.

And finally – and this is where I get all sloppy – I want to thank Bella, my beautiful wife, who has had to put up with me being glued to my computer ever since I discovered the Motley Fool. Also, my even more beautiful daughter Catherine, who was born at the same time as Fool UK, and who will grow up telling all of her friends that Daddy is a Fool.

Nigel Roberts
Chippenham
Wiltshire
December 1999

Appendix 1 – Loadsalinks

No Internet manual would be complete without a list of addresses and sites to look up. The only problem with lists like this is that they're a real pain to use. Things change and they change very rapidly. All of these links were valid at the time of writing, but some of them will have ceased to exist by the time it reaches the bookshops. Don't worry, because we have created a Foolish Resources section at: **http:// www.fool.co.uk/community/resource/** where you can find all these links online. Most of them refer to sites beyond the Motley Fool, for which we can take no responsibility.

Annual Reports
Financial Times Annual Report Service –
http://www.icbinc.com/cgi-bin/ft
Free copies of company annual reports mailed to you. Order online.
CAROL – **http://www.carol.co.uk/**
Free service offering links to company annual reports.
Northcote – **http://www.northcote.co.uk/**
Links to annual reports published by companies on the Internet.

American Depository Receipts (ADRs)
Motley Fool UK – **http://www.fool.co.uk/School/ ADR.htm**
Introduction from a UK perspective
Bank of New York – **http://www.bankofny.com/adr/**
Lots of information on ADRs, with details of all companies listed from around the world which are listed on the US markets, including profiles and links to home pages.
J P Morgan – **http://www.adr.com/**
Probably the best source of information on ADRs.

New York Stock Exchange – **http://www.nyse.com/public/intview/4a/4aix.htm**

Non-US companies listed on the NYSE.
Brokers' Consensus Forecasts
Motley Fool UK – **http://quote.fool.co.uk**
Financial Times – **http://www.globalarchive.ft.com/cb/cb_analysis_comp.htm?**
Hemmington Scott – **http://www.hemscott.com/**

Company Fundamentals
Motley Fool UK – **http://quote.fool.co.uk**
Start at this page.
Yahoo! – **http://finance.uk.yahoo.com/**
Enter the company name or EPIC code to get quote then click on profile.
FT.com – **http://www.ft.com/hippocampus/cobrief.html**
Includes brokers' forecasts.
Wright Company Analysis – **http://profiles.wisi.com/profiles/UnitedKingdom.htm**

Directors Dealings
UK Shares – **http://www.ukshares.com/dd/**
Can be slow in being updated.
Bulletin Board Bugle – **http://www.angelfire.com/al/bbbugle/**
Not a complete service, and again suffers from slow updating.
Investor Ease – **http://www.investorease.com/**
A good up-to-date listing of recent directors deals.

Ethical Investing
Motley Fool UK – **http://www.fool.co.uk/StockFoolery/ethical.htm**
Weekly update on Ethical Investing.
UK Social Investment Forum –

http://www.uksif.org/home/welcome/frameset.shtml
Moneyworld Guides –
http://www.moneyworld.co.uk/faqs/ethfaq3.htm
Frequently Asked Questions on ethical investing
Ethical Investment Research –
http://www.eiris.u-net.com/

Endowment Policies
Motley Fool UK – **http://www.fool.co.uk/
personalfinance/compleat/1999/cp990225.htm**
Fools don't surrender!
Motley Fool UK –
http://www.fool.co.uk/Bribble/1999/Bribble990707.htm
An Expensive Endowment Lesson by Maverick Trader.
Motley Fool UK –
http://www.fool.co.uk/Bribble/1999/Bribble990609.htm
Getting rid of an endowment
Motley Fool UK –
http://www.fool.co.uk/Bribble/1999/Bribble990616.htm
The tale of a sale by BigSD
The Insurance Policy Trading Company –
http://www.endowments-direct.co.uk/
Absolute Assigned Policies –
http://www.aap.co.uk/index.html
Beale Dobie – **http://www.bealedobie.co.uk/home.htm**
The A1 Policy Shop – **http://www.endowments.com/**
Foster and Cranfield – **http://www.foster-and-
cranfield.co.uk/** – Endowment Auction
Neville James – **http://www.neville-james.co.uk/**
Policy Trading Company –
http://www.policytrading.co.uk/
Surrenda-Link – **http://www.surrendalink.co.uk/**

Investment Clubs
Motley Fool UK – **http://www.fool.co.uk/school/
investmentclubs/investclub1.htm**

Proshare – **http://www.proshare.org.uk/**
Non-profit organization which oversees investment clubs in the UK.
Tragic – **http://www.geocities.com/WallStreet/Bureau/4461/**
SKOOPS – **http://www.james58.freeserve.co.uk/index.htm**
Potopisyn – **http://www.potopisyn.freeserve.co.uk/**

Internet Banks
Alliance and Leicester –
http://www.alliance-leicester.co.uk/
Barclays – **http://ibweb.barclays.co.uk/home.htm**
Citibank – **http://www.citibank.com/uk/intbank/index.htm**
Co-operative Bank – **http://www.co-operativebank.co.uk ib_tandc.html**
Royal Bank of Scotland – **http://dbpc.rbos.co.uk/ info_point.htm**
Egg – **http://www.egg.com/**
First Direct – **http://www.firstdirect.co.uk/ Pages/home.html**
first-e – **http://www.first-e.com/uk/index_e4.html**
Legal and General – **http://www.landg.com/**
Lloyds TSB Bank – **http://195.92.18.3/retail/ S01L01_FS.htm**
Nationwide Building Society –
http://www.nationwide.co.uk/
NetMaster –
http://www.norwichandpeterborough.co.uk/intro.htm

New Issues (IPOs)
Financial Mail – **http://www.financialmail.co.uk/ newissues.htm**

Online Calculators
Legal and General Mortgage Calculator – **http:// www.legalandgeneral.co.uk/mgecalcs/repay_java.html**
Work out how much you can afford to borrow.

Times-Money Mortgage Calculator –
**http://www.timesmoney.co.uk/mortgage/calculator/
mortgagecalc1.html**
Work out how much you can afford to borrow.
Universal Currency Converter – **http://www.xe.net/ucc/**
Convert any currency into any other.
What Car used car valuation – **http://www.whatcar.co.uk/**
Calculate the value of your pride and joy.

Quotes and Trading Information
Motley Fool UK – **http://quote.fool.co.uk/**
FTSE International – **http://www.ftse.com/**
Information about market indices.
Market Eye – **http://www.market-eye.co.uk/**

Stock Screening
UK Invest – **http://sites.stockpoint.com/ukinvest/
stockscreener.asp#SCREEN_APPLET**

Taxes
Motley Fool UK –
http://www.fool.co.uk/PersonalFinance/Taxes/taxes.htm
Motley Fool UK tax message board –
**http://boards.fool.co.uk/Messages.asp?id=20400040003
15000**
Chartered Institute of Taxation – **http://www.tax.org.uk/**
Ernst and Young –
http://www.eyuk.com/template1.nsf?Opendatabase
Income tax calculator –
http://www.quicktax.co.uk/tax/calculator.dcg
Inland Revenue – **http://www.inlandrevenue.gov.uk/
home.htm**
Price Waterhouse Coopers – **http://www.pwcglobal.com/
uk/eng/main/home/index.html**
Moneyworld Tax calculator –
http://www.moneyworld.co.uk/cgi-bin/taxcal98/tax_calc

FTQuicken – **http://www.quicktax.co.uk/**
UK Tax Directory – **http://www.uktax.demon.co.uk/**

UK Brokers – Internet Dealing
Motley Fool UK – **http://www.fool.co.uk/personalfi-nance/discountbrokers/discountbrokers1.htm** – Fool's Guide to choosing a broker.
Barclays – **http://www.barclays-stockbrokers.co.uk/**
Beeson Gregory – **http://www.beeson-gregory.co.uk/**
Cave and Sons – **http://www.caves.co.uk/index.htm**
Charles Schwab – **http://www.schwab-worldwide.com/ Worldwide/Europe/ Sterling/**
DLJ Direct – **http://www.dljdirect.co.uk/**
E*TRADE – **http://www.etrade.co.uk/**
Fastrade – **http://www.fastrade.co.uk/**
James Brearley – **http://www.jbrearley.co.uk/**
RedM – **http://www.redm.co.uk/secure/index.asp**
Stocktrade – **http://www.stocktrade.co.uk/**
Share Centre – **http://www.share.co.uk/** (not strictly an Internet broker)
Xest – **http://www.xest.com/**

UK Broker Research
Ellis and Partners – **http://www.ellisandpartners.co.uk/**
Equity Development Ltd –
http://www.equity-development.co.uk/index.html

UK Company Web sites
Link site – **http://www.planetearth.u-net.com/ companies/companies.shtml**
Excellent site put together by a private individual full of links to UK companies. Company sites sorted by index and sectors, plus lots of other great links.

UK Financial News
Motley Fool UK – **http://www.fool.co.uk/news.htm**

AFXPress – **http://www.afxpress.com/**
BBC Business News –
http://news.bbc.co.uk/hi/english/business/default.htm
Bloomberg UK –
http://www.bloomberg.com/uk/ukhome.html
Electronic Telegraph – **http://www.telegraph.co.uk/**
London Evening Standard – **http://www.thisislondon.co.uk/**
dynamic/news/business/top_direct.html
MaxMoney – **http://www.ukmax.co.uk/maxmoney/**
This is Money – **http://thisismoney.co.uk/news.shtml**
News Now – **http://www.newsnow.co.uk/**
The Independent – **http://www.independent.co.uk/**
The Times – **http://www.the-times.co.uk/**
news/pages/Times/frontpage.html?999
The Sunday Times – **http://www.sunday-times.co.uk/**
news/pages/Sunday-Times/frontpage.html?999
Times Money – **http://www.times-money.co.uk/**
UK Business and Financial Review – **http://www.news-**
review.co.uk/FT.com – http://www.ft.com/
Hemscot.net – **http://www.hemscott.net/**
MoneyWorld News – **http://www.moneyworld.co.uk/**
news/
Market Eye News Search –**http://www.market-eye.co.uk/**
scripts/News.dll?SearchNews
NASDAQ UK News – **http://www.nasdaq-uk.com/**
asp/uknews.asp
PA News Centre – **http://www.pa.press.net/business/**
main.html
Reuters – **http://www.reuters.com/news/**
Teletext – **http://www1.teletext.co.uk/business/**
The Economist – **http://www.economist.com/**
UK Invest – **http://www.uk-invest.com/freeserve/**
ITN Online – **http://www.itn.co.uk/**
Pigeon – **http://www.pigeon.co.uk/**

Unit Trusts

Interactive Investor – **http://www.iii.co.uk/**

MoneyExtra-ISA Guide – **http://www.moneyextra.com/ isa/default2.asp**

MicroPal – **http://www.micropal.com/index2.htm**

This is Money – **http://www.thisismoney.com/ukgi1a.htm**

Standards and Poors – **http://www.micropal.com/**

MoneyWorld – **http://www.moneyworld.co.uk/funds/**

Trustnet – **http://www.trustnet.co.uk/general/**

UK Invest – **http://www.uk-invest.com/news/utrusts.html**

Appendix 2
Internet Glossary

ADSL – Asynchronous Digital Subscriber Line – Refers to a technology which allows rapid data transfer down standard telephone lines. Faster downloading than uploading. ADSL allows an 'always on' Internet connnection, meaning no more dialing up.

AOL – America Online – An online information service, which also functions as an ISP. Whether you love or hate what AOL provides, you have to love the stock price of this US-listed company these last few years. It's been ballistic.

Applet – A small Java based program that is embedded within a Web page. Applets are responsible for many of the fancy effects you see on Web sites.

ARPANET – Advanced Research Projects Agency Network – The computer network designed to maintain a workable communications system in the event of enemy missile attack. Developed in the late 60s and early 70s by the US Department of Defence as an experimental network which would survive a nuclear war.

ASCII – American Standard Code for Information Interchange – The effective standard for coding information into binary numbers. In other words, each letter of the alphabet, number and other character is assigned a universally recognized binary number. With the ASCII standard established, it's possible to exchange data between different computers and software. One ASCII character takes up one byte of memory. E-mail uses ASCII text.

Bandwidth – How much information you can send through a connection. Measured in bits-per-second. The larger the bandwidth of a line, the quicker it can transfer data. 'High bandwidth' or 'Broadband' connections are the buzzwords of the moment. Increasingly, you'll hear people using it in general conversation. Thus 'I simply don't have the bandwidth

197

for that', ought to mean 'I'm so insanely busy, I don't even have the time to think about what you're proposing', but often means 'Frankly, darling, I can't be bothered'.

Baud – The measurement used to rate the speed of a modem. It measures how many bits can be sent or received per second.

Bill Gates – The multi-billionaire who started Microsoft. The ultimate geek.

Bit – Binary Digit – The smallest form of computer memory, a bit is either on or off (1 or 0). Eight bits form a byte.

Bitmap – A digital picture, consisting of dots (pixels), with each dot a separate colour.

bps – bits per second – A measurement of how fast a connection will download data. A 28.8 modem can move 28,800 bits per second. The same as Baud.

Broad Band – (see Bandwidth above).

Browser – Software that allows an Internet user to view Web documents.

Byte – A set of bits that represent a single character. There are eight bits in a byte.

Cookie – A piece of information sent by a Web server to a Web browser that is saved on your computer and is sent back to the server whenever the browser makes contact with the server in the future. Cookies often contain information such as login or registration information, your user preferences and the like. Despite what many people believe cookies do not read the contents of your hard disk and send this information to someone else.

Cyberspace – Originally penned by William Gibson in his novel *Neuromancer*. The word Cyberspace is often used to describe the whole universe of the Internet.

Download – The transfer of a file from the server computer to your own computer, or from your own computer to another Web user's computer. An upload is sending a file to the server from your own computer.

Domain Name – The unique name that identifies an

Internet site, such as fool.co.uk. Domain names have at least two parts, separated by dots. The part on the left is the most specific, and relates to the name of the company or Web site, the part on the right is the most general. From the 'bit on the left' you can usually tell quite a lot, for example .co.uk tells you that this is a commercial site based in the UK. The most common extension is .com where .com signifies a commercial company, often, but not always, based in the USA.

E-mail – A method of sending electronic messages, usually text, from one person to another via a computer. Volumes of e-mail across the world are now massive and commerce depends on it.

FAQ – Frequently Asked Questions – Documents that list and answer the most common questions on a particular subject. FAQs are usually written by people to try to prevent the same question from being asked over and over. Most Web sites have some FAQs buried somewhere or other, and the Fool is no exception.

Firewall – A combination of hardware and software that separates a LAN (see LAN below) from the Internet for security purposes. It filters the traffic and only allows through whatever is authorized.

Flame – Abusive messages sent by e-mail, on newsgroups or message boards. Flame wars can break out when users fail to adhere to 'netiquette'.

Flame War – When an online discussion degenerates into a series of personal attacks between the writers, rather than discussion of their positions. Pretty rare at the Fool, we have to say.

FTP – File Transfer Protocol is a standardized protocol for moving files between two Internet sites. FTP is a special way to log in to another Internet site for the purposes of retrieving and/or sending files.

GIF – Graphic Image File format is a common compressed format for storing image files on the Internet.

Hit – A is a single request from a Web browser for a single item from a Web server. The popularity of a Web site is usually measured by the number of hits (or impressions) that it receives.

Home Page – A Web page that is designed as the starting off point of a Web site, also often referred to as front page, or index page.

Host – Any computer on a network that provides services to other computers. Also commonly referred to as a server.

HTML – HyperText Markup Language – The standard language used to define documents for use as Web pages.

HTTP – HyperText Transfer Protocol – This allows Web browsers to retrieve files from the Web servers. That's why traditionally URLs begin with http://. (These days, though, browsers mostly don't require you to insert 'http://' at the start of a URL.)

Hypertext – Any text that contains links to other documents (see HTML above).

Internet – The huge collection of computer networks around the world that all communicate with each other.

Intranet – Private network inside a company or organization which is strictly for internal use.

ISDN – Integrated Services Digital Network – A special kind of digital phone line and service. ISDN does not use a modem, and is able to transfer information at somewhat higher speeds, but nothing like as fast as ADSL.

ISP – Internet Service Provider – A company that provides access to the Internet. In the UK free ISPs have mushroomed since the emergence of Freeserve in 1998.

Java – Java is a programming language invented by Sun Microsystems that is specifically designed for writing programs for use on the Internet. These are downloaded automatically onto your computer and can be run automatically, providing interesting and exciting animated graphics and much more.

JPEG – Joint Photographic Experts Group – JPEG is the most popular compressed format for image files on the Internet.

LAN – Local Area Network – A computer network limited

to the immediate area, usually the same building. Your office probably has a LAN.

Leased Line – A dedicated line that is leased for exclusive twenty-four hours, seven days a week use and can be left permanently open. The highest speed data connections require a leased line.

Login – The process of connecting to a remote computer system, for example to your ISP.

Lurker – Someone who reads a message board, but does not contribute to it. Lurking's OK and is positively encouraged before posting on a new board, so you can get a feel for the place.

Modem – **Mo**dulator, **Dem**odulator – A device that allows you to connect your computer to a phone line, allowing it to communicate with other computers.

Mosaic – The first graphic browser that was available for use on the Web that offered a common interface. *Mosaic* enabled the widespread adoption and popularity of the Web. (See Netscape below.)

Netiquette – The etiquette of the Internet.

Netizen – Derived from the term citizen, referring to a citizen of the Internet.

Netscape – A Web browser and the name of a company, now owned by AOL. The Netscape browser was originally based on the *Mosaic* program. Mark Andreessen and Jim Clarke founded a company called Mosaic Communications, which changed its name to Netscape Communications Corporation in November 1994.

Network – Any connection of two or more computers linked to share resources. (See LAN above).

Newsgroup – An Internet discussion group. Collected together, newsgroups form the USENET.

Node – Any single computer connected to a network.

Password – A secret word used to gain access to a computer, network, the Internet or individual Web sites. It is vital to use passwords that cannot be easily guessed by other people.

It is amazing how many people use simple and obvious pass-words such as their children's or partner's names to protect their most important private information.

Portal – A Web site that is or is intended to be the first place people see when using the Web. Typically a 'Portal site' has a catalogue of Web sites, a search engine, or both. A Portal site may also offer e-mail and other service to entice people to use that site as their main 'point of entry' (hence 'portal') to the Internet.

Posting – A single message posted to a newsgroup or message board.

Search Engine – A Web Site which provides an automated index and hence is the place you go to find things on the Internet.

Spam/Spamming – The use of mailing lists, or message boards, to broadcast unwanted information, usually a business proposition or scam, to a large number of people who didn't ask for it. The term probably comes from the Monty Python sketch which featured a café where every dish on the menu consisted of spam. The manufacturers of Spam, as you can imagine, aren't too pleased.

Thread – An ongoing discussion in a message board, grouped under one heading.

URL – Uniform Resource Locator – The standard way to give the address of any site on the Internet. A full URL looks like this: **http://www.fool.co.uk**

USENET – A world-wide collection of discussion groups, with comments passed among hundreds of thousands, if not millions of individuals. There are over 10,000 discussion areas, called newsgroups.

World Wide Web, WWW, or '**The Web**'. The interlinked network of documents described in HTML and stored on computers across the Internet.

Appendix 3
Internet Shorthand You Need to Know

You'll find long lists of this stuff in various books and on Web sites. To be honest, very little of it is genuinely in regular use in e-mails and on message boards. Below is pretty well all you need to get going. If there's anything else in regular use you need to know, you'll pick it up as you go along.

IMHO – In My Humble Opinion.

BTW – By The Way.

FWIW – For What It's Worth

LOL – Laughing Out Loud

AFAIK – As Far As I Know

CYA – See ya

:-) – Smile

;-) – Wink

:) – Sadness

:-0 – Shock! Horror!

BTW, if you're feeling pretty cynical about these trendy abbreviations and symbols, IMHO they are strangely useful in this electronic medium. They wouldn't have become such a widespread shorthand if they weren't. While the acronyms simply reduce the amount of typing needed, the little symbols (known as 'smilies') are a way of substituting for facial expressions and tone of voice. They work well.

Cookies

'Who stole the cookie from the cookie jar?'
'Number one stole the cookie from the cookie jar.'
'Who, me?!'
'Yes, you!'
'Couldn't have been.'
'Then who?'
'Number two stole the cookie from the cookie jar!'
'Who, me?!'
…
…
Old children's rhyme.

If you ever see 'Ah, come on, have a cookie,' at the top of the Fool log-in page, this indicates that your browser is refusing cookies. To use the Motley Fool Web site at its most effective, your browser must have cookies enabled. If you need to be convinced that this is a safe thing to do, read on.

In order to keep a record of who you are, to avoid having to log on every time, and to make access to all your favourites quicker and easier, the Motley Fool Web site uses what are known as cookies. People who are careful of Internet security often ask us questions about cookies, but are they really a security risk and is fear of them justified?

Here's an extract from an actual question that was asked on the Motley Fool message boards:

Cookies, cookies, cookies
Since starting to use the Internet, everybody I have spoken to tells me to disable the cookies. I usual connect at work where I haven't bothered to do this. (The connection goes through at least three servers and a cache.) Otherwise I would be unable to talk

to you now.

Now, I don't suffer from Orwellian paranoia, but I have failed to find a sensible answer to the question of cookies in any Internet book I pick up. So please can someone help me on this one?

1. In layman's terms, what is a cookie and how does it work?

2. Does the cookie pick up information from my PC and send it back to the originator?

3. Is there any way that, via a cookie, somebody can pick up information that is truly confidential, e.g. name, e-mail address, or even postal address?

We received several great answers to that message, far too many to reproduce here, so here is a response based on all those answers. Many thanks to all those who helped.

1. In layman's terms, what is a cookie and how does it work?

A cookie is a small text file that is sent from a Web site server to your computer when you connect to it. The amount of information in the cookie varies, but never exceeds 255 characters. The cookie contains information that will be sent back to the server on subsequent visits, in order to identify you.

The Motley Fool computers use a database. This database contains information about all registered Fools – favourite features, favourite message boards, last message number read on each board etc, and sufficient information to link you to your database entry is stored in the Motley Fool cookie, loaded onto your computer by the site when you last logged on. Keeping this information in the cookie removes the need for you to log on again every time you access the site.

The information held in cookies is stored in two parts, called the 'key' and the 'value'. The site you're visiting can set both of these – it can tell your browser things like, 'Please store the value "myvalue", under the key "mykey". Later it can ask the browser for the value of a specific key, 'Please tell me what the value associated with "mykey" is.'

If your browser has cookies turned off (or you delete your stored cookies), then next time you reconnect to the Fool site you will be asked for your user name and password in order to identify you, and access your database entry.

2. Does the cookie pick up information from my PC and send it back to the originator?

Your browser can send back information that is stored in the cookie, but it can only send back the cookie that the Web server sent to it in the first place. An individual site can only ask the browser about cookies that it has created itself, and cannot obtain the information from any other sites' cookies.

You should always remember that a cookie is just a tiny fragment of text. It is not a program, so it cannot do any of the nasty things that viruses and their ilk can do.

3. Is there any way that via a cookie, somebody can pick up information that is truly confidential, e.g. name, e-mail address, or even postal address?

No. Information held elsewhere on your computer cannot be accessed via a cookie, and the cookie mechanism cannot be used to access confidential information held on your computer.

Our very own Tom Connor, TMFSki, one of our programmers, had the following to say about how the Motley Fool cookies work too...

I am the techie that did all of the cookie programming, and in the spirit of openness and Foolish honesty let me briefly go over precisely how we are using cookies on our site.

On the first visit to any page on our site we try to write out a temporary cookie with the word 'Welcome' in it ('Hullo' for the UK site). If you accept that cookie, we then overwrite it with a permanent one on the next page you go to. The things we put into this cookie are as follows: a random unique string, today's date, and your user name once you login or register. That's it, pretty simple. Once all this is done we don't touch the cookie anymore or try to send you any more. There are a few exceptions to this, like ads and the search results pages, which also write a few cookies.

So, what does this much-maligned little fellow look like? Here is my Fool cookie:

Fool
USERNAME=tmfski
UID=W31999y1m31d11h31m57s480.5414
FIRSTVISIT=1/31/99 11:31:57 AM
fool.com/

What good is all this? A number of things. It allows us to not waste precious Web page space promoting the virtues of registering for our site if you already have. It also helps us know how many unique visitors come to our site. This is very important for the Marketing type folks and helps determine what we can charge our advertisers, our primary source of income.

Some other notes: Our cookies can only be read by our site, no other site can read them. We can put nothing in them that you have not already told us about yourself, for example your user name. Our cookie is about 150 bytes long, making it smaller probably than any graphic that your browser has downloaded, or about one tenth the size of this message. We can use up to twenty cookies, but have chosen to keep things lean and neat in one cookie. In fact, if you ever had one of our older cookies, we delete it when setting the new one, cleaning up after ourselves.

I hope this information helps. Cookies get a whole lot of bad press (often by the companies that want to sell you some kind of anti-cookie software), but in fact are quite benign.

Fool On and prosper!
TMFSki

www.ingramcontent.com/pod-product-compliance
Ingram Content Group UK Ltd.
Pitfield, Milton Keynes, MK11 3LW, UK
UKHW040640280225
455688UK00002B/35